I AM NOT ASHAMED OF CHRIST

OF CHRIST

Personal Testimonies of a Christian Doctor

I AM NOT ASHAMED OF CHRIST

Personal Testimonies of a Christian Doctor

Dr. R. Peprah-Gyamfi

Thank You Jesus Books

I AM NOT ASHAMED OF CHRIST:
Personal Testimonies of a Christian Doctor

Published by Thank You Jesus Books, an imprint of
GLOBAL VILLAGE PUBLISHERS LTD

www.peprah-gyamfi.com
email: **info@peprah-gyamfi.com**

ISBN: 978-1-913285-42-5

www.peprah-gyamfi.com

CONTENTS

PREFACE

In 2004, I published a book titled "The Call That Changed My Life."In it, I described, among other things, my upbringing in the small village of Mpintimpi, the circumstances surrounding my conversion to Christianity, and the arduous journey I took to medical school. I dedicated a chapter to explain the primary reason for writing the book: to testify to the goodness of the Lord in guiding me from my humble beginnings to medical school in Hanover, Germany.

It has been twenty years since I published that book, and I can affirm that the Lord has continued to reveal Himself in many ways in my life since completing that manuscript.

While I may not possess precise statistics to back up my claims, I can't help but point out a significant concern: there appears to be a noticeable decline in interest in Christianity across the globe, particularly in the developed Western world.

As an ordinary person, I recognize that I cannot change the world on my own. However, I can share my personal experiences with the Lord to help rekindle the faith of believers and lead unbelievers to Him.

The Lord's hands have indeed preserved me from countless dangers.

While my Christian journey has certainly faced its challenges, I can assure you that no matter how tough times got, the Lord has always been by my side.

As I've mentioned, my testimonies are not just a recount of my experiences, but a deliberate effort to instill hope and provide encouragement to you, the reader, in your spiritual journey.

I write for the young convert, whose unsteady legs might waver in life's storms. I write for the battle-torn Christian, who feels overwhelmed by the ferocious attacks of the evil one. I also write for the skeptic, who, due to the evil and injustices in the world, doubts the existence of a loving Father. I understand your struggles, and I'm here to offer hope.

Lastly, I have the atheist in mind. I may not know what has led you to your beliefs, but even if you consider my testimony to be worthless, I can only hope and pray that the Lord touches your life journey so you may come to know His goodness and kindness.

PROLOGUE

"For we did not follow cunningly devised fables"

Sunday, September 17, 1978, marked a pivotal moment in my Christian journey. On that fateful day, I responded to the altar call of Pastor Ofosu- Mensah, the resident pastor of the Kotobaabi branch of the Open Bible Church in Accra, Ghana, and gave my life to Jesus Christ. Just three days earlier, on Thursday, September 14, the Lord had sent His servant, Doris, to share her testimony about the amazing works of the Lord of Hosts in her life. At the end of her testimony, she invited me not only to accept the Lord into my life but also to join her church, which I did.

To this day, I still cherish one aspect of the worship service in my former church: the time allocated for testimonies. This part of the service occurred between the Worship and Adoration segment and the sermon, lasting about fifteen minutes. During this time, worshippers with testimonies were invited to come forward and share their experiences with the congregation.

Often, our dear pastor would humorously interrupt those who exceeded their allotted time with enthusiastic shouts of "Praise the Lord!" to which the congregation would respond with loud cries of "Hallelujah!" These interruptions frequently led to laughter throughout the church. At that point, the person sharing their testimony would understand the cue and promptly wrap up their story. This entire process was carried out with Christian love, and hardly anyone who was interrupted took offense.

I would like to take readers back to a typical Sunday worship service at the Open Bible Church. The Worship and Adoration portion of the service has just concluded. Pastor Ofosu-Mensah has invited anyone with a testimony to come forward, face the congregation, and share their experiences.

About half a dozen worshippers, including myself, responded to the invitation and lined up at the front of the congregation. I patiently listened as others shared their testimonies.

Now, it is my turn to share my testimonies. Before I do so, however, I would like to briefly share some thoughts on one of my favorite verses:

For we did not follow cunningly devised fables when we made known to you the power and coming of our Lord Jesus Christ, but were eyewitnesses of His majesty. 2 Peter 1:16 NKJV

Peter, one of the leading disciples of the Lord Jesus Christ was growing older and was aware that he was nearing the end of his life. This realization weighed heavily on him. He began to reflect on the extraordinary experiences he had accumulated over the years, particularly those related to his time spent following the Lord.

Peter was not just any witness; he was a pivotal one. He had the privilege of walking with the Lord and witnessing His miracles and teachings over approximately three years.

Recognizing the deep importance of the knowledge he possessed, which would inevitably be lost with his passing, Peter made a significant decision. He chose to document his experiences, ensuring that his unique encounters with the Lord would not be forgotten.

Peter lived in a vastly different era compared to our modern age, which is dominated by social media. In his time, capturing and broadcasting events was not as instantaneous or widespread as it is today.

However, people had ways to record events, primarily through writing. Although the process was laborious, involving parchment, ink, and quills, it allowed them to document history.

Peter understood the immense value and importance of the information he held in his memory. He believed it was worth every ounce of effort to ensure his testimonies were captured in writing for future generations, despite the writing challenges of the time.

Peter, who deeply understood human nature and its tendency to doubt what people do not observe for themselves, went to great lengths to emphasize the truth of his testimony.

Good friends of posterity, believe me when I say that I am not fabricating anything here. No, no! Take it from me: this is no myth, no fable, and definitely no fake news. I assure you of my honesty in this testimony. I was there; I saw it with my own eyes. What you are reading is not a cunningly devised tale or a product of my imagination.

The mention of **cunningly devised fables** , takes me back to my childhood in the small village of Mpintimpi. As kids, we often gathered around the elders of our community to listen to their folk tales—stories intricately woven with wisdom and tradition.

Of particular note are the enchanting tales centered around Kwaku Ananse, a celebrated character known for his cleverness and wit. Each folktale featuring Kwaku Anase, opens a door to a world of endless possibilities, igniting the imagination of young minds and inspiring a sense of awe and wonder.

In our village, there was an elderly storyteller whose mastery of folklore was unparalleled. One of his tales resonated deeply with me, leaving an indelible mark on my memory. Our village experienced two distinct seasons: rainy and dry. During the rainy season, the forest that surrounded our homes was teeming with snails, prompting villagers to venture out in search of these delicacies.

As we gathered around Kofi Aworo—that was his name—to listen to his captivating stories during "snail season," he would proclaim that the snails had rained down from the heavens! For years, I accepted this magical explanation without question. It wasn't until much later that I recognized the story for what it was: a whimsical tale meant to ignite our imaginations.

Moving from my childhood days to the present, it is evident that modern technology's has empowered the creation of "cleverly crafted tales". This alarming trend has given rise to fake news, deep fakes, and similar threats that undermine our perception of truth and reality.

No, we did not follow cleverly devised myths created by human minds or modern technology, Apostle Peter emphasizes. What I am testifying to is not a product of my imagination. I witnessed these events with my own eyes and heard the words with my own ears. Indeed, I observed the supernatural transfiguration of the Lord and listened to the voice that spoke to Him from heaven. I was not alone on that occasion; James and John were also present. I am recording my eyewitness account of these extraordinary events as a testimony for future generations. This is not fake news; it is the truth.

While I do not wish to place myself on the same level as the Apostle Peter, one of the leading disciples of the Lord, I want to echo his words—namely, that the testimonies I am about to share are not cunningly devised fables. They are not stories I have invented on my own, but rather real events that have happened to me. Some may consider part or even all of my testimonies as unremarkable and not worth sharing.

I respect the opinions of those who may not find my experiences extraordinary; however, I see them as unique and significant, deserving to be shared with others. I feel a deep obligation to bear witness to these remarkable interventions in my life—interventions that I believe can only be attributed to the Hands of the Good Shepherd of my Soul.

These experiences have significantly contributed to my personal growth and faith journey. I hope they inspire you, dear reader, just as they have inspired me.

CHAPTER 1

The Lord intervening on my behalf even before I knew Him

Initially, I intended to share how the Lord has worked in my life since I made the personal decision to follow Him. However, as I reflected on my life journey, I realized that the Lord's favor has been evident in my life even before I consciously chose to follow Him. At that moment, I recalled a passage of Scripture, specifically John 1:44-48.

Philip, like Andrew and Peter, was from the town of Bethsaida. Philip found Nathanael and told him, "We have found the one Moses wrote about in the Law, and about whom the prophets also wrote— Jesus of Nazareth, the son of Joseph."

"Nazareth! Can anything good come from there?" Nathanael asked.

"Come and see," said Philip.

When Jesus saw Nathanael approaching, he said of him, "Here truly is an Israelite in whom there is no deceit."

"How do you know me?" Nathanael asked.

Jesus answered, "I saw you while you were still under the fig tree before Philip called you."

Just as the Lord noticed Nathanael beneath the fig tree before he came to Him, it struck me with awe that Almighty God was intervening to preserve me from harm even prior to my commitment to Him.

Truly, even before I decided to follow the Lord, His protective arms were actively working in my life, thwarting the Enemy's attempts to derail the plans He had for me. I want to share two powerful testimonies that demonstrate how, just like Nathaniel, "the Lord saw me under the fig tree" long before I came to know Him.

***

I was born into very modest circumstances in the small village of Mpintimpi, located about 160 kilometers (100 miles) northwest of Accra, the capital city of Ghana.

A makeshift bathroom served as the "labour ward," and my mother had to endure severe labour pains without a healthcare professional present to provide pain relief.

However, she was not alone; alongside the traditional midwife assisting her, angels of the Living Lord were there to offer comfort and protection.

Even before I had the chance to familiarize myself with the world I had chosen to enter, something threatened to cut my time here short.

I was barely eight months old when, according to my parent's account, a boil developed on the left side of my neck

A common belief in my culture is that treating boils is not within the scope of conventional medicine. My parents decided, therefore, to resort to traditional medicine. Nevertheless, this showed no sign of being capable of managing the situation. As time went on, the boil grew larger, becoming overwhelming and suffocating. Oh, poor me! It felt like my death was imminent.

Eventually, someone recommended a traditional healer in Afosu, a larger settlement about four miles south of our village, to my desperate parents.

According to my parents, I could hardly breathe when they brought me to the traditional doctor's home. Upon seeing my desperate condition, he immediately left for the woods and returned a short while later with some herbs. He pounded the herbs into a paste and applied them to the boil.

Then came the turning point! Suddenly, as if an invisible hand had used an unseen instrument to cut it open, the boil literally exploded!

Today, I am convinced that the herbal paste applied to the boil didn't make the ultimate difference. As a doctor, I recognize that the abscess harboured billions of bacteria, perhaps trillions. While my parents kept me at home and did not seek medical help, those germs could have infiltrated my bloodstream, potentially leading to blood poisoning—a situation that would certainly have cut my life short.

Surely, the hands of the Almighty Father, the Good Shepherd of my soul, preserved me from the evil machinations of the devil even before I had the willpower to respond to His call on my life.

***

While I was growing up, there was no school in my village. Children of school age had to walk to the Nyafoman settlement, which was a larger community located about two miles north of my village, to attend primary school.

We didn't have access to buses to take us to school. Good health, especially having legs free of disease, was not just a luxury but a necessity in our pursuit of education.

The Evil One specifically targeted one of the legs I needed for my daily walk to school in an attempt to hinder my pursuit of education.

It all began when I was in Year 5 in primary school. Suddenly, and for no apparent cause, my left ankle joint began to swell up. Initially, the discomfort was bearable, permitting me to continue walking the distance to attend school.

In time, however, the pain increased in intensity. Despite the increasing discomfort, I refused initially to stay out of school. I enjoyed going to school and stayed away only when it was absolutely impossible to do so due to ill health. A time eventually came, though, when the excruciating pain left me with no choice but to stop going to school.

Desperate to find a cure for their son, my parents tried various types of traditional medicine. Eventually, they took out a loan and took me to the hospital. Conventional medicine did not lead to an immediate cure, however.

Nevertheless, a little over two years after the onset of my left ankle condition, the pain subsided to the extent that it enabled me to resume my education.

Even though I had not made a conscious decision to follow the Lord at that stage in my life, the Good High Priest was mediating for me before the Throne of Grace.

CHAPTER 2

The call that changed my life

Dear reader, I invite you to pay attention as I share my conversion story. The transformation from a sinner to a believer is truly a miracle.

As I mentioned in the previous chapter, an ailment that affected my left ankle caused a two-year interruption in my education. A few years after I resumed my elementary education, I made significant progress in my academic journey. I passed an entrance exam that allowed me to transition from the village elementary school to Oda Secondary School in our district capital, Akim Oda.

After obtaining my GCE O-levels in July 1976, I progressed to Mfantsipim Secondary School, one of the leading secondary schools in the country, to complete my two-year sixth form.

Founded in 1876 by Methodist missionaries, Mfantsipim School takes pride in being the first secondary school in Ghana. Located in Cape Coast, approximately 140 km (90miles) west of Accra, the school has educated many prominent figures in the country. For a boy from the village of Mpintimpi, gaining admission to this prestigious institution was not just an educational milestone; it's akin to a cleaner's child in the UK securing a place at Oxford or Cambridge – a remarkable leap toward a brighter future!

One Sunday, towards the end of my second and final year at Mfantsipim, rumors began to circulate that a student from the junior classes had gone missing. I heard the news early because the missing student was in my dormitory.

Later, more details emerged: he had left the previous day to visit his girlfriend at a nearby girls' boarding school. Contrary to his usual habit, he had not returned. Since that time, all communication with him had ceased.

The dormitory captain informed the housemaster about the situation. Just before any action could be taken, two police officers arrived at the school to check if anyone was missing. They mentioned that authorities at the main hospital in the city had notified them about an unclaimed body of a young victim from a traffic accident that had occurred the previous evening. Eventually, the deceased boy was identified as the missing student.

Later, more details emerged regarding the circumstances of his death. After visiting his girlfriend, he waited at a bus station to catch a bus to Cape Coast when a saloon car passed by. The driver offered him a lift, but only a few miles into the journey, the vehicle was involved in a serious accident. Our schoolmate was killed instantly.

Although I knew him only casually, his tragic death at the age of about 15 sent shockwaves through me. The sudden realization that life could end abruptly struck me powerfully and gave me much to reflect on.

Before our companion's body was taken to his hometown for burial, a memorial service was held in his honor in the large school chapel. During the solemn service, we were allowed to file past his body to pay our last respects.

This close encounter with the departed boy—the lifeless body of a young person who had just a couple of days before been going about his life—prompted me to ask myself: where would I spend eternity if the same fate were to befall me at any time soon?

As expected, since Mfantsipim Boys was founded by Methodist missionaries, worship services are conducted in the Methodist tradition. Among the hymns we sang during that solemn occasion was Methodist Hymn 157:

Jesus Calls us! Over the tumult
of our life's wild restless sea,
Day by day His sweet voice soundeth
Saying: Christian follow me.

As of old, apostles heard it
By the Galilean lake,
Turned from home and toil and kindren
Leaving all for His dear sake.

Jesus calls us from the worship
Of the vain world's golden store,
From each idol that would keep us,
Saying: Christian love Me more!

In our joys and in our sorrows,
Days of toil and hours of ease,
Still He calls, in cares and pleasures,
That we love Him more than
these.

Jesus calls us! By thy mercies,
Saviour, make us hear Thy call
Give our hearts to Thine obedience.
Serve and Love Thee best of all.

I am not easily swayed by emotions. However, as we sang that song, the words touched my heart, and I could hardly suppress my tears. I began to reflect on the hymn. Although I believed in the existence of God and regularly attended church, I couldn't claim to have a personal relationship or a full commitment to Christ.

The harsh realities of this world had nearly turned me into a skeptic.

The problem of universal suffering in the presence of a loving God deeply troubled me. Whenever something terrible occurred around me, I found myself questioning: if there is a loving God, why is the world filled with so much evil—war, crime, injustice, confusion here, confusion there, confusion everywhere?

On that day, as we were saying goodbye to our departed classmate, I felt a renewed call from Jesus to follow Him.

As we sang, I reached into my pocket, took out a pen, and made a prominent mark next to hymn number 157. That was the only song in the hymn book that had been highlighted in that way.

In the days that followed, the death of my schoolmate weighed heavily on my mind. If something similar were to happen to me, where would I spend eternity? I kept asking myself.

Eventually, life returned to its usual rhythm. I continued attending the Sunday evening worship service, as was required of every student, but without any sincere commitment to leave behind the "world's vain golden store" to follow Jesus, as the hymn urged me to do.

The two-year sixth-form course at Mfantsipim concluded in June 1978. Shortly before we took the series of examinations for the West African Examination Council GCE A-Level certificate, we completed our university admission forms. I chose medicine as my first option, applying to both the university in Accra and the one in Kumasi. At that time, only two of the three universities in the country had medical faculties.

***

After leaving Cape Coast, I first traveled to visit my parents in Mpintimpi. After spending a few days there, I headed to Accra with the hope of finding vacation employment to earn some money before starting my university education in October. I settled in a suburb of Accra called Asylum Down.

On a sunny day, while taking a stroll through the neighborhood, I unexpectedly ran into Doris, an old acquaintance.

She is the cousin of Kwadwo, my best friend and class-mate from Oda Secondary School. I had met her during a previous visit to Kwadwo's hometown, but I was surprised to discover that she lived not quite far from where I was staying.

One day she came for a visit. During the visit, our conversation began with general topics—such as our last meeting in the village, my friendship with Kwadwo, my education, and my plans for the future.

Then came a surprising moment! Turning to me, she asked unexpectedly, "Have you given your life to Jesus the Lord?"

I was startled by her question and, for a moment, I was at a loss for words. "Well," I replied thoughtfully, choosing my words carefully, "I can't say I fully understand what you mean by that. I'm not an atheist; I do believe in God. However, I don't attend church regularly."

"My question is," she said, "have you made a conscious decision to follow the Lord? It's not enough to go to church from time to time. I also used to attend church occasionally, but I was still living a wild life—until I got to know the Lord. Now I am free, free, free!" She smiled. "As the scriptures say, 'If the Son sets you free, you will be free indeed!' Another scripture states, 'For God so loved the world that He gave His only begotten Son, that whoever believes in Him will not perish but have eternal life.'" She looked at me expectantly.

I gazed at her in bewilderment, feeling as though I wasn't fully grasping her words. Although I couldn't consider myself an active Christian, I had a fairly good knowledge of scripture. As I sat face-to-face with her, a thought crossed my mind: "Is Saul also among the prophets?"

She seemed to sense my thoughts.

"Well," she began, "I know for sure that Kwadwo and the others have shared something about me—particularly regarding the wild life I used to lead!"

She smiled, but her words were serious. "Indeed, in the past, I lived to satisfy my flesh. I allowed my desires to dictate my actions. I was a wretched sinner, used by the Devil as he pleased. However, things reached a turning point in my life. I went through a severe crisis."

She noticed my look of surprise. "Oh yes, my life seemed completely shattered. Just at that moment, Almighty God, through mysterious circumstances, called me. I answered His call and gave my life to Jesus the Lord. Now I am free, free, free!"

She continued her testimony for a while, speaking eloquently about her new-found hope and occasionally quoting scripture to emphasize her points. Her eyes sparkled with genuine joy as she spoke—a joy that radiated from deep within her.

Finally, she turned to look me in the eye. "I am inviting you to accept Jesus into your life. I have heard from Kwadwo and others that you are a brilliant scholar. If you give your life to the Lord Jesus, He will use you for His glory." She smiled but spoke earnestly. "Oh indeed, you will never regret your decision to follow the Rock of Ages! If the Lord can change someone like me, He can do the same for you."

She paused for breath and then continued, "Please take some time to think about what you have heard. The Bible says in Revelation 3:20: *'Behold, I stand at the door and knock; if anyone hears my voice and opens the door, I will come in to him and dine with him, and he with me.'*

Today may be your last chance! I don't know if you worship in any church at all, but I want to invite you to worship with us on Sunday. I could stop by on my way to church, so we can journey together."

Once again, I found myself at a loss for words. Eventually, I managed to speak. "You really want me to worship with you?"

"Oh, indeed! The congregation will be glad to welcome you."

"What kind of church is it?"

"It's known as the Open Bible Church."

"Open Bible Church?"

"You've never heard of the Open Bible Church?"

"No."

"Well, it's a Pentecostal church—a truly Bible-based church. You can come and see for yourself!"

"You'll have to give me time to process everything you've told me today!"

"Don't harden your heart, my dear! Today is the day of your salvation; tomorrow may be too late."

At that point, she expressed her desire to leave, but before doing so, she asked me to join her in a short prayer. She prayed that the Lord would open my heart and help break down the last resistance I had within me.

Left alone in my room, Doris's testimony weighed heavily on my mind. I found it surprising that she, of all people, would be the one to speak to me about salvation. I had read and heard about the transformative power of scripture, and I didn't need to look far for a living example of that truth—Doris was truly a testament to its power.

Just then, my eyes landed on my Methodist hymn book, which was resting in one corner of my writing desk. To this day, I cannot explain why I felt compelled to pick it up. As soon as I did, it opened to Hymn 157—the only hymn marked with a tick— the hymn that had touched my heart profoundly just a few months earlier at the funeral of my schoolmate at Mfantsipim. The lines stared back at me, seeming to confront me directly.

Jesus Calls us! Over the tumult
of our life's wild restless sea,
Day by day His sweet voice soundeth
Saying: Christian follow me.

As of old, apostles heard it
By the Galilean lake,
Turned from home and toil and kindren
Leaving all for His dear sake.

Jesus calls us from the worship
Of the vain world's golden store,
From each idol that would keep us,
Saying: Christian love Me more!

In our joys and in our sorrows,
Days of toil and hours of ease,
Still He calls, in cares and pleasures,
That we love Him more than
these.

Jesus calls us! By thy mercies,
Saviour, make us hear Thy call
Give our hearts to Thine obedience.
Serve and Love Thee best of all.

I read through the entire hymn, line by line, and then I read it again. Goosebumps formed all over my body as I absorbed the words. For a while, I could hardly control my tears.

Doris's testimony alone might not have been enough to touch my hardened heart, but the hymn—following so closely after her moving testimony—was the final push I needed.

A still voice within me seemed to say, "The Lord has found you at last. In the past, you ignored the call. This time, there is nowhere for you to run."

An unusual quiet filled the room. Without realizing it, I found myself on my knees, praying. When I stood up, I began searching for a Bible. There were a couple of them in the room, and I picked one up to read various passages from the New Testament. Suddenly, the words reverberated in my heart in a way I had never experienced before.

The next day, I contacted Doris to share my desire to accompany her to church the following Sunday. As I had expected, she was delighted to hear the news! We arranged for her to stop by our home on her way to church. Together, we would take a *tro-tro* (a commuter mini-bus) to the church, which was located about three miles away.

I accompanied her to church the following Sunday as planned. Pastor Ofosu-Mensah delivered a powerful and heartfelt sermon during my first visit. At the end of the service, he made an altar call, and I did not hesitate to respond. Eventually, a few others and I were invited to come forward to the altar to be prayed for. After he prayed for us, he congratulated us on our decision. Amid cheerful applause and shouts of "Welcome home! Welcome home!" we returned to our seats.

CHAPTER 3

The dream of promise

And it shall come to pass afterward, that I will pour out my spirit upon all flesh; and your sons and your daughters shall prophesy, your old men shall dream dreams, your young men shall see visions

Joel 2:28

Before the Lord called me, I, like everyone else, had dreams. Naturally, my dreams did not stop once I became a Christian.

I can however testify that after the Lord called me under the circumstances already described, some of my dreams turned out to be prophetic in nature. In this chapter, I am sharing a particular dream that proved to be prophetic.

In the previous chapter, I recounted the events that led to my conversion. As I mentioned, I had just completed my GCE A- Levels at the time. My goal while taking those exams was to do well and gain admission to one of the two medical schools in the country.

One might ask, "Why did you want to study medicine?"

My desire to pursue a career in medicine was born during my childhood in my birth village, Mpintimpi. The human suffering I witnessed as a child significantly influenced my decision. The nearest hospital was located about 30 km (20 miles) away. Due to the widespread poverty, residents typically sought medical help at the hospital only as a last resort.

Even if they managed to raise the necessary funds for transportation and to cover the expected hospital bills, getting the sick to the hospital remained a challenge. The road connecting Mpintimpi and Nkawkaw was rarely traveled, making it difficult for the sick to find transportation to the hospital.

Additionally, the villagers were small-scale farmers who relied on what they grew for food. Accompanying someone to the hospital could result in a full day's loss of work on their farms, and there were no government agencies to compensate them for this loss.

Due to the factors mentioned above, many individuals who fell ill often waited at home and tried traditional remedies before seeking conventional medical treatment. Unfortunately, in some cases, it was too late for them to be helped by the doctors.

These adverse conditions, which negatively impacted healthcare access for the community, motivated my decision to pursue a career in medicine. I wanted to make a difference. I envisioned operating a mobile clinic that would allow me to drive around the neighbourhood and provide healthcare services to those in need.

***

Immediately after my conversion, I was filled with a burning enthusiasm to serve the Lord. I faced two options: to go directly to Bible School and become a pastor, or to first pursue my long-held dream of becoming a doctor, and then serve the Lord in whatever capacity He deemed appropriate.

Ultimately, I chose the second option for one main reason: I did not want to financially burden the church I might pastor in the future. I have nothing against pastors receiving financial support from their churches. However, I was inspired by the example of the Apostle Paul, who worked as a tentmaker to support himself and did not want to overburden the young churches he founded.

Neither did we eat any man's bread for nought; but wrought with labour and travail night and day, that we might not be chargeable to any of you: Not because we have not power, but to make ourselves an ensample unto you to follow us. For even when we were with you, this we commanded you, that if any would not work, neither should he eat.
1 Thessalonians 3:8–10

I believed that the Lord had blessed me with the mental aptitude to study medicine, but what I lacked was financial support. Fortunately, during that time, Ghana's educational system was very supportive of prospective students. Tuition was free up to the university level, and the government provided free accommodations and meals for students. Additionally, students had access to generous state-backed loans to help purchase textbooks and other educational materials. Therefore, even though my parents were impoverished, I had a good chance of making it to medical school once I obtained the required grades.

I lived on a street in Accra, near the home of my sister, who introduced me to Christ. Since we lived close to each other, we interacted regularly. We took the same commuter bus to church, met for prayer and Bible study, and engaged in various daily activities, such as shopping together.

Over time, she shared her immediate plans for the future with me. Her brother lived in Germany, and her sister-in-law, who had grown fond of her, was planning to invite her to Europe. She hoped that while she was in Germany, she might have the opportunity to settle there indefinitely.

About two weeks after my conversion, when I was literally on fire for the Lord, I encountered my first disappointment as a Christian. This disappointment was related to my A-level results. Although I passed all four subjects, my performance fell short of my expectations. I was unable to achieve the excellent grades I had hoped for, which would have guaranteed me automatic admission to one of the two medical schools in the country.

Ultimately, the university offered me admission to pursue a course in General Science. Although I accepted the offer, I viewed it as a temporary solution, a sort of plan B, while I continued to work towards achieving plan A.

As I grappled with this unexpected turn in my academic journey, I reconnected with a good acquaintance of mine in October 1978. Upon hearing about my failure to gain admission to medical school in Ghana, he promised to leverage his connections with the Ghana–Soviet Friendship Society to help me secure a scholarship to study medicine in the Soviet Union. The selection process was set for early January 1979, and he assured me that he would do every-thing possible to ensure I became a beneficiary of one of the several scholarships provided by the communist country.

To provide some context, this was during the Cold War era. The countries of the Eastern Bloc offered hundreds of scholarships to developing countries in Africa, South America, and Asia, enabling their citizens to study in those nations. These scholarships were allegedly offered without any strings attached. However, the donors hoped that after their lengthy stay in their respective countries, the bene-ficiaries would return to promote communist ideology in their home countries.

Although I knew I might not find other Christians to fellowship with while in the Soviet Union, I was eager to pursue my path to medical school. I was convinced that if it was God's will for me to study there, He would also help me maintain my faith during my time there.

***

At the time I made the conscious decision to follow the Lord, I had not yet been baptized. A few days before Christmas in 1978, I underwent water baptism with other church members at a popular beach in Labadi, Accra.

Filled with the enthusiasm and fire of a young convert, I chose to dedicate the period between Christmas and New Year to fasting and prayer.

After a long night of prayer, I retired to bed. Was I asleep or just half-awake? One thing I know for sure is that I was not fully conscious. Suddenly, a scene flashed before my eyes—it was so vivid that I can still recall it very clearly to this day.

In this dream, I found myself walking down the street of a settlement that looked like any other village in rural Ghana. The dusty streets were lined with mud houses topped with corroded corrugated iron roofs. Just as I was walking along the street, Doris, the sister who had led me to Christ suddenly appeared out of nowhere.

Startled by the unexpected meeting, she exclaimed with excitement evident on her face: *"Peprah! At long last, we've finally met in Europe!"*

In that moment, I returned to reality. I looked around—the room was completely silent. The walls started to feel familiar, and it dawned on me that I had been dreaming.

Such a revelation, which came during a period of fasting and prayer, convinced me without a doubt that the Lord was revealing future events to me. I began to wonder how Doris and I could meet in Europe.

Regarding my sister in Christ, her sister-in-law, who is a German citizen, was making the necessary arrangements to help her settle in Germany. She had promised to assist her in obtaining a visa and to cover the cost of her flight.

I speculated that I would be studying in the Soviet Union. Those who had received similar scholarships informed me that they were allowed to travel to the West during holidays. I planned to take advantage of this opportunity to visit my sister in Germany. This, I thought, would fulfill the prophecy.

It seemed that the prophecy would indeed be fulfilled in the way I just outlined when I was initially selected for the Soviet scholarship. The plan was for the successful candidates—around two dozen of us—to depart for the Soviet Union in August of that year.

Just as I was coming to terms with the prospect of leaving Ghana later that year to begin my studies, I received unexpected news six weeks after my selection: my name had been removed from the list! My disappointment was immeasurable.

I was determined not to accept this decision without a fight. In the following days, I reached out to several prominent members of the Ghana-Soviet Friendship Society, including the national president, to plead my case. Unfortunately, my efforts were in vain.

Just when it seemed that everything was working against me, my Christian sister's situation was improving. After facing some initial challenges, she finally managed to join her relatives in Germany in February 1980.

For a while, it seemed impossible for the prophecy from my dream of meeting my sister on the streets of Europe to come true. She was in Germany while I remained stuck in Accra, and my dream of studying medicine felt shattered.

Just as I was about to give up hope of seeing the prophecy fulfilled, I unexpectedly ran into Gyasi, an acquaintance I had met during a visit to Kwadwo's hometown. As readers may recall, Kwadwo was my best friend and classmate in secondary school. The last time I saw Gyasi, he was still in Sixth Form and had expressed his desire to study architecture after completing his GCE A-levels.

During our meeting, he mentioned that he would be leaving for Nigeria in the next few days. He planned to look for work in Lagos, to help him secure an air ticket to join his brother in the U.S. His ultimate goal was to study architecture there.

I decided to accompany him to Nigeria. On my part, I would work to fund my journey to Germany, where I hoped to pursue my goal of studying medicine. My Christian sister, who was already settled in Hamburg, promised to do what she could to assist me if I made it there.

Upon my arrival in Nigeria, I was initially compelled to take on various odd jobs at construction sites to make a living. Eventually, I secured a position as a secondary school teacher. After working in Nigeria for about sixteen months, I managed to save enough money to book a flight to what was then East Berlin. From there, I intended to continue on to West Berlin, but my plans to travel straight to Hamburg were not immediately feasible.

During this time, Germany was divided into communist East and capitalist West due to the Cold War. Because West Berlin had a unique status as a capitalist enclave within communist East Germany, I required a visa to travel from

West Berlin to my sister in Hamburg, which is located in West Germany. Without this visa, I had no choice but to remain in West Berlin.

Driven by my dream of becoming a doctor, I researched the requirements for admission to medical school in Germany. I discovered that the chances of a foreigner like me gaining admission were nearly nonexistent. However, I was not discouraged; instead, my determination to pursue this seemingly impossible goal only grew stronger.

Recognizing that knowledge of the German language was essential to achieving my goal of studying medicine in that country, I dedicated myself to learning it.

Lacking the financial resources to attend a language school, I taught myself instead. My hard work paid off. In a surprising turn of events, the Hanover Medical School offered me admission in October 1983. Unfortunately, my status as an asylum seeker led immigration authorities to deny my request to travel from West Berlin to Hanover to begin my studies.

I was devastated by the news I received. However, amidst this bleak situation, a glimmer of hope appeared on the horizon when the university promised me a second chance the following year.

The university fulfilled its promise. This time, I was able to travel from West Berlin to Hanover, and I ultimately enrolled in the Hanover Medical School in October 1984.

On my way from West Berlin to Hanover, I made a detour to Hamburg on September 4, 1984, to visit my sister. Nearly six years after the prophecy had been revealed to me, we finally "met on the streets of Europe"!

CHAPTER 4

The Lord paving a way where there was no a way

Earlier in my narrative, I mentioned my childhood dream of studying medicine to improve healthcare in my community. After my conversion, I resolved to pursue that dream and use my position as a Christian doctor to further the cause of my Lord and King.

After missing the opportunity to study medicine in Ghana, I sought an alternative route that would enable me to pursue my dreams in the Soviet Union; regrettably, that opportunity also slipped through my fingers.

Around this time, Doris, the Christian sister I mentioned earlier, moved to Germany. I learned from her and some acquaintances living there that it was theoretically possible for me to study medicine in that country. They informed me that university tuition was free for both German nationals and foreigners.

While students must cover their living expenses—such as boarding, lodging, stationery, and other related costs—they can supplement their income by working during vacations, my sources added.

With that in mind, I set off from Ghana on December 1, 1980, heading to Nigeria with the determination to secure employment. My primary objective was to earn enough money to buy a plane ticket to Germany, where I could pursue my dream of studying medicine.

After enduring the challenging conditions in Nigeria for just over seventeen months, I finally left the country on the evening of May 11, 1982, arriving in West Berlin the following afternoon.

However, my hopes were nearly dashed upon my arrival in Germany when I discovered that the optimistic picture painted about my chances of gaining admission to medical school was overly idealistic.

Although tuition was free for both international and domestic students, there were several challenges I needed to overcome to gain admission. The most significant challenge was my lack of proficiency in the German language, as every foreign student was required to provide proof of above-average knowledge of German.

Another major hurdle was financial. Even though tuition was free, I had to present a certificate of financial guarantee from a credible source to demonstrate that I could cover the recognized average monthly living expenses for students.

An additional and considerable challenge I faced in my pursuit of medical school admission was the fierce competition. As one would expect, entering a prestigious field such as medicine comes with rigorous competition, making the journey to acceptance all the more daunting.

The final and perhaps most daunting obstacle hindering my aspiration to gain university admission was my immigration status. After seeking advice from knowledgeable sources, it became clear that the chances of an asylum seeker like me being granted the opportunity to change my immigration status for educational purposes were exceedingly slim.

When considered together, the cumulative effect of these obstacles cast a shadow over my educational aspirations, diminishing the prospect of gaining admission to pursue my cherished degree to almost zero.

Even though the chances of gaining admission to medical school were slim, I refused to give up in the face of what seemed like insurmountable obstacles. Instead, I committed to doing everything within my power to achieve my goal. I placed my trust in Almighty God, believing that if it was His will, it would come to pass.

As my first step, I began learning the language. Since I did not have the funds to enroll in a language school, I realized that self-teaching was my only option, and I embraced the challenge wholeheartedly.

After five months of dedicated self-study, I was finally ready to take the German language test required for my university application.

Thankfully, a Ghana-related organization based in West Berlin agreed to lend me the funds I needed for the test, which I successfully passed with credit.

Regarding the letter of financial support required for the application, the Lord touched the hearts of Kurt and his wife, Karen (more about them later), to provide me with the financial guarantee certificate.

Eventually, I applied to approximately ten German universities for a chance to study medicine. I must admit that I submitted my applications more for the sake of trying than with any real hope of being selected by any of them.

When the universities started responding, it seemed to confirm my fears. Rejection letters poured in, one after another. Just as I had begun to reconcile myself with this reality, one day a letter arrived that looked different from the others. It was, in fact, a large brown envelope.

With trembling hands, I opened it. On pulling out the contents, my heart nearly stopped beating. The feeling of being selected by the prestigious Hanover Medical School was overwhelming.

When Almighty God opens a door, no one can shut it. The events that unfolded after I received my admission letter are a testament to this truth. The immigration authorities initially refused to grant me permission to travel from West Berlin to Hannover to begin my studies. They even suggested that they could persuade the university to deny me the opportunity entirely.

Fortunately, the university stood firm in their commitment to allow me this incredible opportunity. Though I was unable to start my studies in the academic year beginning October 1983, they graciously reserved my place for the following academic year. Ultimately, I was able to make my way to Hannover that year, and for that, I am truly grateful.

Those interested in a detailed account of my journey from my small village of Mpintimpi in Ghana to medical school in Hanover, Germany, are highly encouraged to check out my book, "The Call That Changed My Life."

CHAPTER 5

The Lord guiding me through medical school with just €1,000

In the previous chapter, I shared how the Lord transformed a seemingly impossible situation, ultimately securing my admission to Hannover Medical School in 1984. Thus, after spending about two and a half years in West Berlin, I left the divided city and headed to Hanover.

During my time in West Berlin, I occasionally worked as a cleaner in the homes of families and individuals, as well as in residential homes for the elderly. From my earnings, I managed to save 2,000 Deutsche Marks, which is approximately 1,020 Euros. This amount was all the financial resources I had at my disposal when I began my studies.

It is unnecessary to mention that I could not depend on the remittances from my poor parents in my beloved village, Mpintimpi, to finance my university education in Germany!

At that time, as it is now, tuition at German universities is free for both citizens and non-citizens. While students do not have to pay for lessons, they are responsible for covering the costs of accommodation, food, books, and other miscellaneous expenses related to their studies.

At the time I began my studies, it was generally held that the average student needed 700 DM (approximately 360 Euros) each month for sustenance. Thus, at the start of my studies, the resources available to me could only support me for three months. Yet, I didn't succumb to panic or anxiety about my financial future. I held onto my unwavering faith in Almighty God, who had guided me from my humble village in Africa to a medical school in Germany. I trusted that He would meet all my needs. And He did, in ways that surpassed my wildest expectations!

Please pay attention, dear reader, as I narrate the mysterious ways the Lord, my Provider, worked through various individuals, organizations, and institutions to provide for me during my time at Hanover Medical School.

American Lutheran Church in Berlin: During my time in West Berlin, I attended services at the American Lutheran Church. Early in my stay, I found a leaflet inviting visitors to join their services. I contacted Pastor Gary, who kindly provided me with directions to the church. I continued to attend services there for the rest of my time in the city.

Shortly after I arrived in Hanover, Gary shared some unexpected news with me: the congregation had decided to offer me financial assistance in the form of a stipend of 300 DM every quarter. This generous gesture, which I hadn't anticipated, pleasantly surprised me.

Kurt and Karen: Kurt was the pastor of a German Lutheran church, which was a sister church to the American Lutheran Church. Occasionally, the two churches would come together for joint services. It was during one of these gatherings that I got to know him.

Kurt played a key role in my university application process by providing a written declaration of financial support in case I gained admission—it was a vital piece of paperwork that I needed to provide before any university would consider my application.

Upon my admission, Kurt effectively decided to back his words with action. Shortly after I arrived in Hanover, I received a letter from him with a cheque for 400 DM enclosed. He mentioned that this was just the beginning. He and his wife, Karen, had decided to support me with a monthly payment of 200 DM until further notice.

Ilse: During my hospital admission due to a left ankle condition I met Ilse, a Christian physiotherapist. As I mentioned earlier, the condition had afflicted me for several years. It worsened during my first winter in Europe, which ultimately resulted in the need for surgery.

While alone in the hospital, far from home, I found solace in reading Scripture. This caught the attention of Ilse, who was amazed to see someone reading the Bible in public. I was surprised by her reaction, as reading the

Bible openly wouldn't raise an eyebrow in my home country of Ghana. Meeting her was truly a blessing. Eventually, she introduced me to several German Christians, who also became a source of support for me.

Ilse provided me with monthly remissions of 100 DM over a considerable period after I enrolled at the Hannover Medical School.

Rhea: Rhea was a retired Christian doctor whom I met through Ilse; she sent me regular monthly remittances of 100 DM.

Friedo: He was a pastor at a Lutheran church in Hanover and was a good acquaintance of Kurt. After I moved to Hanover, Kurt reached out to Friedo on my behalf. Ultimately, Friedo's church provided me with financial support of 100 DM each month.

Gottfried: My first address after moving from West Berlin to *mainland* West Germany was in Langenhagen, a town on the outskirts of Hanover.

This led Friedo to introduce me to Gottfried, the superintendent pastor responsible for that district of the German Lutheran Church.

Gottfried and his wife, Sabine, welcomed me into their home with open arms. "You can consider yourself part of our family. In the worst-case scenario, if you cannot pay your rent, you can stay with us!" they assured me.

In the end, Gottfried devised a plan: he opened an account for me and launched an appeal for support from members of his congregation as well as his many acquaintances. From that account, he made a monthly payment of 200 DM to support me.

Anonymous donor: For an extended period, I received significant monthly donations from an anonymous source. Eventually, I discovered that the source was a member of Gottfried's congregation. He preferred to remain anonymous because he didn't want "the whole world to know" he was helping me.

Income from Interpreter Job: As if the assistance I was receiving through His grace weren't enough, the Lord led me to an additional source of income!

One day, shortly after I began my studies, I was contacted by the head of the international students' office at the medical school. She revealed that the police were urgently seeking an interpreter for Twi, which is my mother tongue.

They had arrested a woman who was trying to enter the country with what they suspected was a forged Ivory Coast passport. The police believed she might be from Ghana, but they faced a significant problem: she did not speak any European language. The deadline for holding her without charges was approaching quickly, so they needed an interpreter to assist with the case as soon as possible.

I agreed to travel to the police station where the woman was being held, located about 100 kilometers east of Hannover. At the end of my assignment, the officer preparing the invoice asked about my hourly rate.

"I have no idea," I replied.

"Well, Twi, your native language is considered an exotic language, which commands a higher rate. The interpreter we usually rely on charges 70 DM per hour. However, since you are not certified, you will be paid 50 DM per hour."

I could hardly believe what I was hearing! At that time, the German minimum wage was around 10 DM per hour. To think that a first-year medical student could earn an hourly rate comparable to that of his professors—what a pleasant surprise!

That first interpreter job opened up a world of opportunities for me. Over a considerable period of time, I received invitations to interpret for the police, the courts, and immigration authorities. The part-time interpreting duties became a consistent source of additional income.

Scholarship Award: In my third year, I was fortunate to be guided by divine intervention to a more stable source of income. I received a scholarship from the Friedrich Ebert Foundation, which is associated with the German Social Democratic Party. This program aims to support international students and is not politically motivated.

At that point, I sent a "thank you" note to the individuals and churches supporting me. I informed them of this new development and asked them to withdraw their financial assistance.

Through what I believe to be the mysterious workings of God, the financially struggling student I had been at the start of my studies became very well-supported.

A good year-group friend of mine by the first name of Khosro, an Iranian of the Muslim faith, who I kept in the loop regarding my various sources of income, one day looked me in the eye and began: 'Hey, Robert, your Jesus is very generous to you! He seems indeed to be giving you everything you ask Him for!'

"Well, you have yourself noticed how magnanimous He is!

Accept Him into your life, and He will do the same, if not even greater, for you."

"You want to make me a Christian?" He shook his head.

CHAPTER 6

With one eye through medical school

Ipreviously mentioned that the Lord has been watching over me even before He called me. For instance, He saved me from a potentially life-threatening abscess that developed on the left side of my neck when I was barely a year old.

However, that was not the end of my challenges. As the reader may recall, during Year 5 of primary school, I faced a condition that affected my left ankle, which led to a two-year interruption in my education. Just as the enemy thought he had succeeded in disrupting my academic journey for good, the Lord stretched out His arms and restored the health of my afflicted leg, enabling me to resume my education.

Ah, if only the forces against me would leave me alone to live my life in peace. But no, the Evil one did not relent in his efforts to jeopardize the Lord's plans for my life.

It was the very week I stepped into the world of medical school, going about my daily routine, when I was suddenly confronted with a startling discovery. Dark spots began to invade the field of vision in one of my eyes (I prefer not to disclose which one).

Despite being on the brink of my medical studies, I took on the role of a doctor and conducted a self-examination. I closed my unaffected eye to assess the extent of my impairment. To my dismay, I realized that my vision was blurred in the affected eye. I then attempted to read from a book I was holding. Although the writing was visible, it was so blurred and deformed that I couldn't make out what was on the page!

"Hey, my eye! I have yearned for years to go to medical school, and now you choose to desert me at the very beginning of my journey." The emotional weight of this setback was immense, threatening to derail my long-held dream of becoming a doctor.

Next, I closed the affected eye and read with the unaffected one. To my relief, I could see with perfect clarity. I offered a prayer of gratitude for the blessing of sight, even if it was only in one eye.

I promptly sought medical attention. The doctors were baffled by their findings, as they discovered a scar had formed on the back of the affected eye, specifically in the crucial area necessary for sharp and detailed vision.

"How did that happen?" I asked.

"We believe it was caused by a specific infection. Do you recall having a systemic infection—one that affects the whole body rather than a localized area or organ—that could have led to this?" the doctors asked me.

"Pardon me," I replied. "In the place where I grew up, I was exposed to so many infections that any one of them could have caused it."

"Well, you are right," they acknowledged.

"What is the solution?" I inquired.

"Well, we will do what we can to get to the bottom of the matter," they replied.

This marked the beginning of an extensive investigation into my condition. I had been confident that the advanced German diagnostic tools and the highly regarded German doctors would help find a cure for my condition. Unfortunately, that was not the case. The doctors informed me that the scar, already referred to, was irreversible.

"Were there any tablets that could help?" I asked in desperation.

"No," they replied.

"What about surgery?"

"That is also not possible," they told me.

I thought about the situation for a while. If I had contracted the infection earlier, why did the symptoms only appear at that moment—right when I was about to start my studies? It felt almost comically ironic that just as I was beginning my medical education—a time when clear eyesight was essential—I had effectively become one-eyed!

I earnestly sought healing from the Lord. As my condition persisted, I found solace in the impactful words of the Apostle Paul in 2 Corinthians 12:7-9:

"Therefore, in order to keep me from becoming conceited, I was given a thorn in my flesh, a messenger of Satan, to torment me. Three times I pleaded with the Lord to take it away from me. But he said to me, 'My grace is sufficient for you, for my power is made perfect in weakness.'"

It is generally believed that Paul had a medical condition—possibly an eye condition. He diligently prayed to the Lord Jesus for healing. In response, he received a message that may have sounded like this: "Paul, don't worry about the condition that is afflicting you. Just carry on with your life. My grace is sufficient for you, for my power is made perfect in weakness."

I presupposed that the Lord had a similar message for me. So instead of worrying about my eye condition, I decided to carry on with my life and trust that He would handle it in the way He deemed best.

As I write these lines in June 2025, it has been over 40 years since my eye condition first appeared. The enemy tried to undermine my efforts and my ability to study medicine at the beginning of my studies. However, through the capable hands of my Lord and Savior, the enemy's plans came to nothing.

Not only did I manage to complete medical school with one functioning eye, but by His mercy, the Lord has also strengthened and improved my vision in my other eye. This has enabled me to go about my life without impairment, more than 40 years after the problems first manifested themselves.

CHAPTER 7

A well-timed help from an unexpected source

During my time as a student in Germany, a German friend invited me to his wedding in his hometown, which is about 95 kilometers (60 miles) west of Hanover, where I lived. I planned my journey to ensure that I would arrive about an hour before the start of the ceremony.

I rented a car for the trip. The vehicle was only six months old, so I was confident it wouldn't have any mechanical issues. However, as I was about twenty minutes away from my destination, I heard a strange noise coming from the back of the car. I pulled over on the relatively quiet road and, to my dismay, discovered that one of the back tires had punctured, likely due to driving over a sharp object.

I assumed that the nearly new vehicle would be equipped with a spare tire and the necessary tools to change the damaged tire. However, I had no idea how to do it!

This was in the mid-80s, long before mobile phones became widely used.

Telephone points were installed along the main highways for motorists in need of assistance. However, the road I was driving on was a minor road, and there were no such points in sight, if there were ever any.

Just as I began to feel helpless before the problem, I spotted a vehicle approaching from the direction I was heading. My relief was palpable when the driver didn't just drive on, but pulled to a stop.

"That is one of the unfortunate things that can happen to a driver!" he began.

"Yes, indeed, particularly when you are just a few kilometers from your destination!" I replied.

"May I help you fix the problem?"

"That is very kind of you! To be honest, I have no idea how to do it!"

Soon, he went to work changing the damaged tire. He could definitely be considered an expert, as he completed the task in no time at all.

"Goodbye and safe travels!" He shook my hand and headed back to his vehicle. Moments later, he was out of sight.

Thanks to his timely intervention, I arrived at my destination just in time for the ceremony. My friend was proud to have his African friend there. He wanted me to be part of the festivities because he believed I would add an international flair to what would otherwise have been a purely

German event. I can only imagine how disappointed he would have been if I had arrived late or missed the event entirely!

CHAPTER 8

A God-sent angel to my timely rescue

Though it happened several years ago, the incident I am recounting always causes goose pimples to run all over my body.

I was a second-year student at Hanover Medical School in Germany, residing in one of the three hostels built around the medical school compound to accommodate part of the student population.

In two of the three hostels, each tenant had a small room equipped with a bath and toilet facilities. However, the rooms lacked kitchen amenities. Instead, each floor had a spacious kitchen with several electric stoves and refrigerators, allowing residents to cook their meals and store their food items.

The third hostel where I stayed featured a unique design. It consisted of several apartments, each with two bedrooms. The two tenants in each apartment shared a common living area, which included a built-in kitchen in one corner. Additionally, there was a small enclosure that contained a shower and a toilet.

When I moved into the flat, Roland a fourth year student, a German national, was occupying one of the rooms. Later, I learned from him that he had switched to studying medicine after nearly completing a degree in physics and mathematics.

Each of the two bedrooms had a plug socket for a telephone, which meant I could apply for my own telephone number. However, we agreed to use Roland's number and share the phone bills to save money.

Roland demonstrated his mathematical skills in a practical way by developing a formula to calculate the share of the monthly phone bill each of us was responsible for, based on the line rental and the actual units used.

My routine during the week was to eat at the student canteen, while on weekends, I prepared my own meals. Most often, I prepared fufu, which is undoubtedly the most popular dish in Ghana. For those who may not be familiar with it, let me provide a brief description.

In Ghana, fufu is traditionally prepared by pounding boiled plantains and cassava in a wooden mortar until it achieves a thick, doughy consistency. However, Ghanaians living in the diaspora, particularly in Western countries, have found innovative ways to make fufu. They often substitute the main ingredients—plantains and cassava—with powdered potato and powdered starch, respectively.

Once the fufu reaches the desired consistency, it is shaped into balls. Diners use their fingers to pinch off a small portion from the ball, dip it into soup, and swallow it. This process of pinching, dipping, and swallowing continues until the entire portion is consumed.

The soup, which is a versatile component of this dish, can be prepared in several ways. It may include creams made from palm or groundnut, as well as mixtures that incorporate tomato paste and ground pepper. Typically, meat, fish, or a combination of both is added to the soup during cooking.

One Saturday, after preparing a delicious meal of fufu, I decided to save some of the soup in the fridge for a meal the following day.

As was my custom, I attended church the next day.

Upon returning home around 2 in the afternoon, I set out to prepare another fufu meal. After preparing the fufu balls, I removed the soup from the fridge, heated it on the electric stove, and served some to the fufu balls.

After enjoying my meal, I realized there was still enough soup left for another serving. Therefore, I decided to keep it in the fridge for a later date. However, it was still hot, so I resolved to let it cool down before placing it back in the refrigerator.

Not long after my meal, I began to feel tired, so I decided to retire to my bed—not primarily to sleep, but to rest for a while. As I mentioned earlier, it was a Sunday afternoon. Like most residents of the hostel, Roland had gone home for the weekend and was not expected back until late in the evening.

Before long, the heavy meal took its toll, and I soon found myself drifting off to sleep.

What I didn't realize as I went to lie down for a while was that I had forgotten to turn off the electric stove on which the soup was still simmering. As I lay there, deeply asleep and possibly snoring loudly after my heavy meal, the electric stove continued to heat and boil the soup that had been left on it.

I am using my imagination to envision what happened to the boiling soup while I was fast asleep. Over time, the water slowly evaporated, leaving behind the solid ingredients—meat, fish, and vegetables. Soon, they began to scorch, sending thick fumes wafting through the living room.

For reasons I still cannot explain, I had closed the door to my bedroom before heading to bed. This spared me from the fumes, as there was hardly any space between the carpeted floor and the bottom of the door. However, the main door to the flat allowed the fumes to escape through the gap beneath it, spreading throughout the corridors of the third floor where our flat was located.

If it had been a working day, when people were usually coming and going from the hostel, someone would almost certainly have noticed the fumes. Roland might have been around too. However, it was a Sunday afternoon, and as already mentioned, most residents, including Roland, were visiting their families.

So, as I lay in my bed snoring, the soup burned fiercely on the stove, nearing the point of exploding and potentially setting the room—and possibly the entire building—on fire.

One might wonder whether there was a fire alarm system in the flat. In a large multi-storey apartment building, there are typically alarm systems installed at various points throughout the structure. However, it appears there was no fire alarm within the flat itself; if there had been, it would likely have been triggered during the incident.

Thank God that heaven does not require an artificial fire alarm system to be alerted about fires raging in our homes. Surely, our omnipotent and omnipresent God is present wherever His children are and is always ready to send His angels to rescue them from danger.

As I lay peacefully snoring in my bed, completely unaware of the imminent danger posed by a fire raging in the living area of our flat, the Lord, my Shepherd, initiated a rescue plan in Heaven to save me—unworthy as I am—from harm!

Suddenly, I heard the sound of a phone ringing, almost like something out of a dream. It quickly dawned on me that it was our phone. I sprang out of bed and hurried toward it. The scene that greeted me when I opened the door to my bedroom is still vivid in my memory: the soup dish was engulfed in bright red flames, and thick smoke filled the entire living room.

The shock on my face was unmistakable as I dashed to the stove and turned it off. I swiftly removed the flaming dish from the stovetop and placed it in the washbasin

The thick smoke severely impaired my vision, but I managed to reach the phone, which was still ringing.

"I want to speak to Roland," the caller began after the initial greetings.

"He has travelled home for the weekend," I replied.

"Please tell him his friend Peter called. Let him know that I misplaced his number. That is the reason I have been out of touch for some time. I just stumbled upon it a few minutes ago while I was tidying up my room. I decided to try it right away to see if it was still active."

"That's fine. I will let him know you called," I said.

After placing the receiver back on the phone, I began to reflect on the conversation I had just had. To the caller, it may have seemed like a mere coincidence that he found his friend's lost telephone number and decided to call him. However, I believe that in the grand design of the God of Heaven and Earth, there is no such thing as chance.

The Lord, the Good Shepherd, knew my situation and prompted Peter to make the call at that critical moment to save me from impending catastrophe.

CHAPTER 9

The unseen hands of the Good Shepherd shielding me from disaster

In the summer of 2007, my wife Rita, our three children, and I visited our home country of Ghana. Since our kids were all born in Hanover, this was a unique opportunity for them to connect with their heritage and experience the culture of their parents' homeland for the very first time.

After spending a few days in Accra, we decided to travel to the countryside to visit our relatives. Our first stop was Mpintimpi, a name that should be familiar to readers.

From Mpintimpi, we continued on to Mim, Rita's hometown, situated approximately 400 km (250 miles) northwest of Accra.

After spending two weeks with Rita's relatives, we concluded our journey and headed back south. Our final destination was Accra, where we were scheduled to take our return flight to the UK.

We planned to stop in Kumasi, Ghana's second-largest city, located about 145 kilometers (90 miles) southeast of Mim. We intended to visit my friend Kwasi, a doctor, and his family before continuing to our final destination.

The road we were driving on was single-track. Initially, the terrain was generally flat. However, after about half an hour of traveling through the low-lying countryside, which was characterized by typical green tropical vegetation, we were in for a surprise as the landscape began to change.

Instead of flat land, we encountered rugged, towering mountains with their peaks shrouded in mist. As the landscape transformed, the straight, low-lying road turned into a thrilling challenge, featuring winding hairpin bends, steep ascents, and sharp slopes.

As we reached the bottom of a steep decline, we approached a steep rise. To improve traffic flow for vehicles heading uphill, the road was widened at the base of the incline, creating a dual carriageway for those ascending. This dual carriageway only served vehicles traveling toward the mountain.

Traffic moving down the slope was limited to a single track or lane.

This stretch of road featured well-defined markings, which was a contrast to many other roads in the country that lacked proper signage. Two bold, continuous white lines in the middle of the road indicated that vehicles in each direction should remain within their respective lanes.

Additionally, several white arrows were painted on the road to clearly indicate the intended direction of traffic.

The traffic on the stretch of road we were travelling was sparse; indeed, we hardly encountered any vehicles for a while. When we began the steep climb, ours was the only traffic on the road.

After driving for a while, I noticed that we were approaching a bend about a hundred meters ahead. Until that moment, I had instinctively stayed in the middle lane, which had been a direct extension of the single-track lane I had been on before it became a dual carriageway.

Then, just a few meters before the bend, the realization struck me that there were actually two lanes available for our direction. This insight prompted me to move from the middle lane to the outer lane.

Moments after I switched from the middle lane into the outer lane, a large tipper truck suddenly appeared around the sharp bend, driving alarmingly in the middle lane, which was supposed to be off-limits for oncoming traffic!

Even today, it remains a baffling mystery why the driver chose to travel in a lane that was beyond his limits. The lane designated for him was clear; he wasn't blocked by a slow-moving vehicle, nor was anyone chasing him. So why did he decide to veer into a lane that was off-limits, particularly at a bend? Could it have been a momentary lapse in judgment, a subconscious desire for risk, or simply a mistake?

The thought of what could have happened if I hadn't made that split-second decision to change lanes still sends shivers down my spine. There would have barely been enough time for me to swerve and avoid a potential catastrophe that could have turned our vehicle—and us—into a heap of wreckage.

Even if I had managed to react quickly and swerve away from the truck, the sharpness of that maneuver likely would have resulted in a loss of control. The vehicle could have plunged deep down the mountainside, and I shudder to think about what might have happened to us, the occupants.

There is no doubt in my mind whom I owe my deepest gratitude to for the miraculous outcome of that harrowing situation. The all-powerful and ever-present God, noticing the imminent danger threatening me and my family, sent His angels to our rescue. With their unseen hands, they took control of the vehicle and guided it safely to the outer lane, just in time to avoid a head-on collision with the truck.

Thankfully, the rest of the journey was smooth and uneventful. After a restful night with my doctor friend and his family, we continued our journey to Accra without any further problems.

CHAPTER 10

First adversity, then a humbling gift

As already pointed out, in October 1984, I began my medical studies at Hanover Medical School. Before moving to Hanover, I spent approximately two and a half years in West Berlin as an asylum seeker. During my time in Berlin, I attended the American Lutheran Church, which served the English-speaking American civilian community as well as other English-speaking residents from various parts of the world.

This period was during the Cold War when Germany was divided due to the aftermath of World War II, and several American soldiers were stationed in West Berlin. It's important to note that the American Lutheran Church was not part of the military establishment.

After enrolling as a student at the medical university, I applied for a room in one of the three hostels designated for medical students. Unfortunately, there were no vacancies at that time, so my name was added to the waiting list.

With the assistance of Pastor Gottfried Kawalla, the superintendent pastor of the German Lutheran Church for the Hanover-North district, I found temporary accommodation in a hostel primarily for students from a nearby theological seminary.

Upon moving into my new address, I discovered that there was also a facility nearby that served as a refuge for delinquent teenagers who could no longer live with their parents.

To make moving around easier and save money on public transport, I bought a brand new bicycle. My silver-coloured bike quickly became a great companion, helping me arrive at the lecture hall on time, transport my shopping basket home, and take me to the church I attended, about three miles from the hostel. Like everyone else living in the hostel, I locked my bike to a designated stand near the building every evening.

Barely three months after acquiring my bike, I left my room one morning to collect it for a ride to campus, completely unsuspecting. As usual, I had carefully calculated my time to be punctual for my lectures. However, to my utter dismay, my faithful companion was nowhere to be found! In my desperation, I searched the compound around the building, hoping someone had deposited it somewhere after using it for a ride—yet to no avail! My bike had vanished as if it had been swept away by the wind. I suspected that a resident of the hostel for delinquent youths had sneaked into the bike stand during the night and stolen it!

At that time, I was part of a Bible study and prayer group led by Pastor Kawalla. When the members learned about my situation, one of them offered me a replacement bike. Although it was an old, worn-out bike that couldn't compare to the one that had been stolen, it was comforting to me to know I had a way to maintain my independence from public transport.

A few days later, I rode the bike to church and secured it with a metal chain to a lamppost a few yards from the building. After a lively church service, I returned to retrieve the bike for my ride home, only to discover, to my utter disbelief, that it was gone! I couldn't believe my eyes. Why would someone want to steal a bike that looks so worn-out? It puzzled me.

So, I lost two bikes in less than two weeks. I found myself tempted to be angry with God, especially since I lost the second bike while attending church.

However, I wasn't new on my Christian journey. Indeed over the past several years since my conversion, I had experienced the work of the Great Redeemer in my life. During that time, He had transformed several seemingly dead-end situations, often in ways that exceeded my understanding. With that in mind, I was confident that He would surely find a way out of my unpleasant situation.

As I stood by the lamppost where my bike was supposed to be, I began to think about my next move. I knew my limited financial resources wouldn't allow me to replace the lost bike with a brand new one. Even if I had the money, the events of the past few days made me hesitant to invest a significant amount in a replacement, only to possibly fall victim to theft a third time.

In the end, I decided to visit the flea market in our area at the next opportunity to find a cheap replacement.

However, before I went down that route, I thought it might be a good idea to call Gary, the pastor of the American Church in Berlin. I wanted to inform him of my situation and ask if he could announce it in church the following Sunday, inquiring if anyone might be willing to part with an old bike that was collecting dust in their cellar or back-yard. Gary promised to help with my request.

A few days later, I received a message from Berlin indi-cating that one of the members of the church was willing to present me with a bike. Another church member, who was traveling to Hanover, which is about 290 km (175 miles) west of Berlin, agreed to bring it along.

The gift I received from Berlin continues to humble me. This was no ordinary bike; it was nothing short of extraor-dinary! A pristine, bright red six-gear sports bike that had never been used, it represented a remarkable act of gener-osity—potentially worth three times the price of my first stolen bike. The thought that someone would selflessly give away such an incredible gift was simply beyond my understanding.

The couple who donated the bike had served in the US military in Berlin. They initially brought the bike to Germany, thinking they would need it, but that turned out not to be the case. As their tour of duty in Berlin was ending, they were considering how to dispose of the bike before returning home. After hearing the announcement, they didn't hesitate to donate it to someone they had heard many positive things about.

Even as I write this account, I am still amazed by the mysterious way the Lord led me to this incredible bike.

CHAPTER 11

An alarming incident at a pedestrian crossing

I have truly lost count of how many times the Lord has protected me from danger. I don't intentionally put myself
in harm's way; that would be reckless, like deliberately
driving through a red light. However, when I find myself
in difficult situations despite my best efforts, the Lord, my
shepherd, has been quick to preserve me from trouble, as
the following example illustrates.

The city of Hanover, where I attended medical school,
boasts a well-developed public transportation system,
including buses and streetcars, as well as an adequate infra-
structure for bicycles.

When I arrived in Europe, I did not have a driver's
license. Since the public transportation network was excellent and the bicycle paths were well-maintained, along with
my limited financial resources, taking driving lessons was
not a priority for me.

I moved to Germany in 1982, and in 1988, I returned to Ghana for the first time since my arrival in Europe. During my visit, my older brother Ransford taught me how to drive.

To prevent myself from forgetting or losing my driving skills upon returning to Germany, I decided to continue practicing and obtain a German driver's license. After approximately six weeks of both theoretical and practical driving lessons, I earned my driver's permit in early 1989.

Until that point, my bike had been my main mode of transportation in the city. However, I decided to improve my driving skills and increase my mobility by getting a small used car. Ultimately, I purchased a used Volkswagen Beetle for a very low price.

One day, I drove home from my lectures along one of the city's main roads. Trams or street cars travel down the centre of the road on rails embedded in the street, with traffic flowing in opposite directions on either side of the tram lines.

A tram heading in the same direction as me sped past as I drove. It stopped about 100 metres ahead, and while the passengers were getting off, I caught up with it.

I didn't need to continue driving along the main road the tram was travelling; instead, I had to take the branch road that split off just before the concrete platform unto which the tram passengers alighted.

There was quite a good deal of human activity happening just in front of me—passengers alighting from the train and those eagerly hurrying to board the train, their anticipation palpable in the air.

The pedestrian traffic light just ahead of me, at the entrance of the branch road was green for traffic.

Just a few metres before I reached the pedestrian crossing, the traffic light turned red for vehicles and green for pedestrians. About half a dozen individuals who had been patiently waiting for the green light stepped onto the street.

Upon seeing the red light, I promptly engaged the brake pedal. Under normal dry conditions, there would have been ample braking distance for the vehicle to come to a safe halt before the pedestrian crossing.

To clarify the term "breaking distance" for those who may not be familiar with it: breaking distance refers to the distance a vehicle travels from the moment the brakes are applied until it comes to a complete stop. This distance is affected by various factors, including the vehicle's speed, road conditions, and the overall condition of the vehicle.

However, the situation was different because it had just started to rain, which made the road surface slippery. As I had learned in driving school, such conditions significantly increase the risk of skidding and extend the vehicle's braking distance.

To my utter astonishment, the vehicle didn't stop as expected but instead continued to move forward! In a matter of moments, I found myself driving through a pedestrian crossing, the path filled with unsuspecting humans.

Sensing the imminent danger, everyone on the street reacted with lightning speed, doing whatever they could to avoid a potential collision—running, jumping, and hopping away from the path of the moving vehicle.

Miraculously, every one of them escaped unharmed!

Eventually, my vehicle stopped a couple of metres beyond the traffic light.

Initially, I thought some pedestrians would return to my car to confront me about the scary situation. Happily, apart from a few staring at me and directing insulting gestures, they all walked away.

Even now, when I recall the incident, it sends shivers down my spine. The fact that everyone escaped unharmed is still beyond my comprehension.

Some might attribute the favorable outcome of this incident to chance or luck. However, similar to the near-miss accident involving our bus and a truck in Ghana, I firmly believe that divine intervention saved the day. I feel that Almighty God sent a host of angels to my aid, pulling each of the pedestrians to safety and protecting me from harm and trouble.

The timely intervention of the Good Shepherd saved me from serious trouble. At that time, my driving license was issued on a two-year probationary basis, and I was only a few months into that probation. The consequences could have been even more severe if any pedestrians had been injured or killed. I could have faced a lengthy prison sentence, which would have ultimately jeopardized my studies.

CHAPTER 12

Warding off demonic attacks in Jesus' name

One day, during a visit to my native Ghana in 2011, I suddenly began to experience a peculiar sensation in my head, difficult to describe. It felt like a burning sensation, similar to what one feels in the mouth after eating a hot, spicy meal made with chili pepper. This burning sensation soon developed into a heat that engulfed my entire head and spread to the rest of my body.

As if that were not enough, shortly after these strange symptoms began, I felt as if someone were shaking my heart, causing it to swing like a pendulum. Moments later, it felt like my heart was jumping to and fro in my chest, much like the excitement one feels when receiving good news. Soon, my heart was racing and "jumping around," accelerating rapidly.

The abnormal activity of my heart soon made me feel dizzy and unwell. Moments later, I could barely keep my balance on the chair I was sitting in, as the world around me began to spin before my eyes! I felt as if I were about to collapse onto the floor.

Summoning all the strength I could muster, I managed to reach the bed, which was just a few centimeters away. Meanwhile, I was beginning to feel short of breath. I feared I might not make it to the next day.

The hotel was far from the nearest hospital, and the main roads leading away from the hotel were congested for most of the day. I estimated it would take about an hour to reach the nearest hospital. Meanwhile, my weird symptoms continued to worsen instead of improving.

At that moment, I decided to consult the only doctor available at any time and place—the Greatest Physician of all time; yes, the Doctor whose healing powers know no bounds.

With all the strength I had left, I began to pray: "Save me, Lord Jesus; save me, Lord Jesus; in Your mighty Name, save me!" I recited these lines repeatedly for several minutes.

About half an hour after the onset of the symptoms, I noticed a gradual improvement in my condition. The heat in my head and body began to lessen in intensity. Although my heart was still racing, it was not beating as fast as before. Finally, about an hour after it all began, I felt strong enough to sit up in bed.

The Lord is my shepherd, I shall not want... though I walk through the valley of the shadow of death, I will fear no evil, for thou art with me; thy rod and thy staff they comfort me!" Thus I encouraged myself with these words from Psalm 23.

After sitting for a while, I decided to lie down again. Soon, I was overcome by sleep. When I woke up, it was just past midnight, and all my symptoms had disappeared.

I spent several minutes reflecting on my experience. As a physician, I found it challenging to understand the unusual set of symptoms I had just encountered. Until that moment, I had enjoyed excellent health and could not recall a time in the previous 25 years when I had felt so unwell that I missed lectures or work.

During my visit to Ghana, I had been feeling well, and that was true for that day as well. What then was wrong with me? I kept wondering.

A few days after the health episode I just described, I returned to the UK.

I thought that the unusual health issue would never happen again, but it did—multiple times, as I would soon discover.

One afternoon, while I was working at a prison, I had just settled behind my desk around 2 PM to begin a clinical session. I was about to call in my first patient when I suddenly felt unwell. The familiar symptoms struck me again, and I had to be rushed to the Accident and Emergency (A&E) department in an ambulance.

One moment, I was the one in charge—the doctor making decisions for my patients. The next, I found myself lying on a hospital bed, now the patient waiting for answers and relief. It was a jarring transition, to say the least.

After undergoing several tests in Accident and Emergency (A&E), I was discharged approximately six hours later.

To investigate the potential underlying causes of my condition, I decided to travel to Germany, where I still had medical insurance coverage, to undergo a comprehensive medical examination. Following extensive checks, nothing unusual was detected.

At that point, I began to suspect something I had feared all along—that I was under a demonic attack, and I felt this suspicion was now confirmed.

The Christian sister who led me to Christ once shared that Satan does not respond to diplomatic language. She explained that as a child of God, one must confront Lucifer and the demonic forces aggressively, not relying on their own power, but rather shielded by the authority of the Cross.

That was exactly what I resolved to do. I was determined to take the fight to the Devil, not by my might, but in the mighty name of the Lord, the true source of my strength.

With the advice of my beloved Christian sister in mind, I declared: "Hey, principalities and powers working against me, I declare in the mighty name of the Lord Jesus Christ that I will never allow myself to be intimidated! Yes, I declare in the blood of my Lord and Savior Jesus Christ that you must depart from me and go to hell, where you belong!"

And so it happened! From that moment on, the strange symptoms left me. As I write these words in June 2025, almost fourteen years later, I can honestly say I have never felt those odd symptoms again. As far as my general health goes, I can assert without exaggeration that I am as fit as a fiddle!

CHAPTER 13

A narrow escape from a potentially devastating collision

During my post-graduate training, I secured a job at a clinic in Bad Soden-Salmünster, a town in the German federal state of Hesse, located approximately 310 kilometers (190 miles) south of Hanover. I would leave home on Sunday evenings, stay in rented accommodation during the week, and return home on Friday evenings.

On a typical Friday evening, I set off for home for the weekend. After driving for about an hour on a less busy road, I merged onto the bustling Bundesautobahn 7 (A7), which is known to be the longest highway in Germany. The section of the highway I entered had four lanes in each direction and traversed mountainous terrain. The landscape featured winding curves, slopes, and steep climbs that alternated rapidly.

As expected on a Friday evening, a time when the roads are typically filled with traffic, the highway was bustling with commuters like me returning home for the weekend. There was no speed limit on that stretch of highway. After driving in the second lane for a while, I found myself stuck behind a vehicle moving slower than the average speed of other drivers. To avoid the risk of a collision, I decided to switch to the third lane.

Before carrying out the maneuver, I observed the traffic behind me for a while through the rear-view mirror to ensure it was safe to do so. However, I neglected to consider what I had learned in driving school about blind spots. I was cautioned not to rely solely on the rear-view mirror to check traffic behind and around my vehicle, but also to use the side mirrors and turn my head to look over my shoulder.

In any case, I failed to take these additional precautions and changed from the second lane to the third lane without realizing that there was a vehicle just a few metres away from me in that lane.

Even now, I still wonder how the driver of that vehicle managed to avoid a collision by quickly swerving into the fourth lane, which thankfully had enough space for such a maneuver.

I can hardly imagine what would have happened if that vehicle had collided with mine. It would, without a doubt, have resulted in a multi-vehicle collision of unimaginable proportions, likely leading to multiple fatalities, including perhaps myself.

Sometimes, I feel as if Almighty God has not just assigned me a single guardian angel, but legions of them to watch over me throughout my life!

CHAPTER 14

A frightening wildlife encounter in a tranquil setting

It was a chilly autumn morning, around 5:50 AM, and still quite dark. I was driving along a dual carriageway in an isolated area of northern Germany, heading to a town approximately 145 kilometers (90 miles) west of Hanover for an appointment. I had left home early to ensure I arrived on time for the meeting.

The section of the road I was driving on passed through a forest reserve, with no signs of human activity on either side—just dense vegetation. Nature appeared to be at peace in the lush green scenery before me.

Alone in my vehicle on this isolated road, nearly devoid of traffic at that early hour, I felt as if I had landed on a planet far away from the troubled world I was accustomed to.

At one point, I felt myself starting to doze off. To avoid falling asleep at the wheel, I reached for the radio knob and switched it on. Soon, my vehicle was filled with the voice of a newsreader, broadcasting some of the distressing events happening in our world.

After listening to the radio for a while, my attention shifted to the day's busy schedule ahead of me. After the meeting, I needed to drive back to Hanover as quickly as possible to attend another meeting in the afternoon.

Then, in an instant, it happened! A deafening bang erupted from the front of the vehicle on the driver's side, shattering the tranquility. The force of the impact sent the car into a spin; for a moment, it seemed that control would slip from my grasp. Yet, I somehow managed to wrestle the vehicle back under control and bring it to a halt. Stunned and disoriented, I stepped out of the car to uncover the mystery behind the impact.

The sight of blood on the road was a grim clue—it was a wildlife collision. I began to look around for the culprit. Soon, I spotted the lifeless body of a deer on the hard shoulder, about twenty meters ahead of me. What a massive creature it was; indeed, a giant of its kind!

After identifying the cause of the problem, I began inspecting the damage to the vehicle. I noticed a significant amount of fuel leaking from the engine compartment, which suggested that the engine had been damaged. Unfortunately, this turned out to be true.

Additionally, there was considerable damage to the driver's side of the vehicle, which had taken the brunt of the impact, and the windscreen was also cracked.

Despite the extent of the damage, I initially decided to try starting the engine and driving to the nearest service station. However, the engine failed to start.

Ultimately, I called the German Automobile Club (ADAC) for assistance. They helped me by towing my vehicle to the nearest available garage. I was provided with a courtesy car, allowing me to continue my journey and arrive at my destination just in time for my appointment.

Speaking of insurance—the vehicle had the benefit of comprehensive insurance, insurance cover that took care of the material costs.

It turned out that the engine had suffered significant damage and needed replacement, along with several other components. Thankfully, my vehicle was covered by comprehensive insurance, so I didn't have to worry about the costs.

While my vehicle was insured through a standard earthly policy, I also felt a sense of protection from a higher source—Divine protection—that ensured I did not come to harm. I have heard stories of serious accidents involving wildlife, such as deer, that resulted in multiple casualties among the occupants of those vehicles. However, thanks to the protective arms of my Lord and Savior, I emerged from the scary incident unscathed, without a single cut, bruise, or any pain.

CHAPTER 15

A dramatic fall that nearly ended in disaster

Towards the end of 2023, I decided to venture into film-making by adapting some of my books into films. My first project, "Legacy Africa," was based on a book of the same title. I took on the role of the lead actor in the film, and some scenes were shot in my native Ghana.

One memorable scene required me to stand at a mountain top with a panoramic view of lush green vegetation in the background.

The site for filming the scene was accessible via a rugged, dusty road that was rarely traveled. Due to the poor condition of the road, we decided to park our vehicles at the base of the mountain and walk to the filming spot. One group chose to walk along the dusty road, while I joined another group that opted for a bush path.

At the end of the filming session, some members of the team decided to walk down the mountain using the dusty road already referred to. They invited me to join them. I decided against taking that path. Instead, I chose to join the group that was walking back along the rugged bush path we had taken earlier.

I had assumed that the descent would be easy after the challenging ascent, but I was in for a surprise.

As I started walking down the steep slope, I quickly realized that the incline was steeper than I had anticipated. The momentum soon became overwhelming, pulling me down further than I expected. Before I could do anything about it, I lost my balance and fell hard onto the bare ground.

What I haven't mentioned yet is that there was a small mango plantation at the bottom of the mountain. As I fell, I landed just a few centimeters away from a mango tree! In fact, my head narrowly missed crashing into it by only a few centimeters.

Members of the team who had chosen to descend the mountain with me rushed to my aid.

"Are you alright, or do we need to take you to the hospital?" my director asked, clearly concerned.

"No, I'm fine. A guardian angel has taken care of me," I replied.

"Really? You have a guardian angel?"

"Yes, I do! In fact, not just one, but several! I've lost count of how many times Almighty God has dispatched them to my rescue, delivering me from various precarious situations."

CHAPTER 16

A Miraculous Escape on a Holy Thursday

*B*ut now thus saith the Lord* that created thee, O Jacob, and he that formed thee, O Israel, Fear not: for I have redeemed thee, I have called thee by thy name; thou art mine.

> *When thou passest through the waters, I will be with thee; and through the rivers, they shall not overflow thee: when thou walkest through the fire, thou shalt not be burned; neither shall the flame kindle upon thee.*
>
> *For I am the LORD* thy God, the Holy One of Israel, thy *Saviour: I gave Egypt for thy ransom, Ethiopia and Seba for thee.*
>
> *Isaiah 43: 1-3*

On April 8, 2025, I woke up with a vivid dream etched in my memory, as if it had just unfolded. The clarity of the details was so striking that it felt almost unbelievable to consider it just a dream.

In the dream, I found myself lying on a trolley in what appeared to be a surgical theater. The identity of the hospital remained a mystery even after I woke up.

A group of individuals surrounded me, all dressed in green uniform. There was a sense of urgency in the air, and the faces of those around me displayed a mix of concentration and concern, reflecting the gravity of the situation.

One of the people surrounding me tied a tourniquet around my upper arm and began to lay an intravenous line (IV line). Although I could see my veins bulging, the individual appeared to struggle to find one due to my darker skin tone.

I no longer recall exactly what had necessitated the impending surgery. Just then, I woke from the dream and realized I had been asleep.

The first words that came to my mind were: "Hey, Satan, the arch-enemy, I curse you in the blood of Jesus! Whatever you and your host of demons are planning against me has been neutralized in Jesus' Name."

At that moment, I recalled what I had learned from Pastor Ofosu- Mensah, the beloved pastor of the Open Bible Church I mentioned earlier. He taught us that the Lord often communicates with us through dreams.

He shared that there are times when God illuminates the Devil's schemes against His children through dreams. This revelation serves as a reminder that our Heavenly Father has already thwarted these plans, keeping us vigilant and aware of the spiritual battles He is fighting for us.

With this in mind, I concluded that the Lord, my Shepherd, had already thwarted the enemy's evil plans against me. He chose to reveal the Devil's schemes to help me remain vigilant against Satan's intentions.

The events that occurred just a week after the dream would validate my thoughts.

***

On Holy Thursday, April 17, 2025, Rita and I embarked on a heartwarming journey to Germany to reunite with our beloved children, Karen and Jonathan. Our entire family had relocated from Germany to the UK in 2006, but they have now returned to Germany for work.

Even before Karen and Jonathan moved back, visiting Germany had been a cherished tradition for us. On average, we make this journey four times a year.

***

Before I continue my narration, I would like to provide a brief overview of the geographical position of the British Isles in relation to mainland Europe for those who may not be familiar with it. Understanding this geographical context will help clarify the events I'm about to narrate.

The United Kingdom is an island located on the western edge of mainland Europe. Historically, the only ways to access the United Kingdom or the British Isles from the mainland were by sea or air.

Traveling from the British Isles to continental Europe by sea typically involves driving your vehicle onto a ferry in Dover, a port town in the United Kingdom, and being transported across the English Channel to the continent.

***

After many years of planning, construction of a tunnel beneath the English Channel at the Strait of Dover began in 1988 to establish a rail link between the United Kingdom and France. The Channel Tunnel, also known as the Eurotunnel, was a game changer when it officially opened on May 6, 1994. Stretching 50.5 kilometers (31.4 miles) and reaching a maximum depth of 75 meters (250 feet), it provides a convenient and comfortable way to travel to the UK.

The tunnel accommodates high-speed Eurostar passenger trains and Eurotunnel Shuttle trains, which transport vehicles using a roll-on/roll-off system. Travelers drive their cars to Folkestone in England and Calais in France. Upon arrival, they drive their vehicles onto the train and park them there. Car owners and their passengers must remain in their vehicles during the crossing, which typically takes about 35 minutes.

My first experience with the Channel crossing was in December 1999 when I drove with my family from Germany to visit my brother Ransford in London.

Since moving to the UK, we have preferred road travel when visiting Germany. Our main reason for this is our love for certain German foods that are not readily available in UK shops. Driving our car allows us to fill it with a significant amount of various German food items.

Although we have the option to take the ferry, we prefer using the Eurotunnel to cross the English Channel to mainland Europe.

On April 17, 2025, we set off from home at around 11 a.m. to begin our journey. We traveled in our 7-seater Renault Espace, a spacious family vehicle we acquired about ten years ago. Initially, we chose this car to accommodate our family of five.

Although our children no longer live with us, we decided to keep the vehicle primarily for its extra space, which is useful for transporting items back to the UK during our visits to Germany. As I just mentioned , we have a fondness for certain German food items that are not easily obtainable in the UK.

The first leg of our trip was the approximately 310-kilometer (190-mile) drive from our home in Loughborough, in the British Midlands, to the coastal city of Folkestone. The sun was shining, and the air was filled with the scent of fresh grass as we drove through the picturesque British countryside. The drive took about three and a half hours and was incident-free.

After undergoing the usual passport checks, we joined an Eurotunnel train for the Channel crossing, which also went smoothly.

Finally, we drove off the shuttle train and emerged in France. As is customary, just before leaving the train, the drivers were reminded of the crucial need to drive on the right side of the road, which is standard in continental Europe.

After a half-hour drive through northern France, we seamlessly crossed into Belgium. Thanks to the Schengen Agreement, border checks between EU countries are a thing of the past. A simple sign welcomed us to Belgium, marking the transition from one country to another—a process so smooth it's almost imperceptible.

After about an hour's drive through Belgium, we stopped at a service station. It has become our custom to stop at this particular station for two main reasons: to fill up our fuel tank and because Rita has developed a liking for a special type of cake they sell there.

The stop at the service station lasted about twenty minutes. Finally, we resumed our journey, with a little over 120 kilometers left to drive to our final destination, Kaarst, a picturesque town on the outskirts of Düsseldorf known for its charming streets and delicious local cuisine.

After a smooth thirty-minute drive from the service station, we crossed the Belgian border into the Netherlands without any issues. The transition was so seamless that, similar to our journey from France to Belgium, the only signs indicating we had entered a different country were the welcoming signposts and the differing designs of the traffic signs.

Our route took us through a region of the Netherlands near the German border, and it took less than an hour of driving to reach the frontier between the two countries.

Finally, after about ten hours of travel from home, we entered Germany. Our final destination, Kaarst, was only about thirty kilometers away. I began to envision our arrival and the joyful reunion with our children.

I obtained my driving license in Germany after under-going extensive theoretical lessons and robust practical training. After receiving my license, I drove regularly on the roads for over fifteen years before moving to the UK. Needless to say, I am familiar not only with the roads but also with the driving styles of the average German road user.

It was an exceptionally dark night, and I found myself needing to adapt to the reduced visibility, as German high-ways lack the bright illumination of those in the countries we had just traveled through.

We were about a twenty-minute drive from home and needed to exit the highway we were on to take another one that would lead us directly to our destination.

"Take the exit!" the Sat Nav instructed me. Although I was familiar with the route and typically didn't need assis-tance, I decided to keep the Sat Nav on since we had started our journey together.

I gently steered right, leaving the main road to enter the exit that would lead us to the highway heading home. A quick glance at the Sat Nav screen indicated that I needed to drive about half a kilometer along the exit road before merging onto the other highway.

I thought I could continue straight for a short distance before making a slight right turn to merge onto the highway toward our final destination. Then it all happened! Suddenly, out of the darkness, a red-and-white striped metal barrier loomed just a few meters ahead. It was a heart-stopping moment when I realized I was on a direct collision course with the metal structure, which rose to a height of about a meter!

I instinctively slammed the brake pedal, but it was a futile attempt.

The vehicle collided with the metal barrier in a deafening crash, instantly crumpling the front. The air was filled with a thunderous noise, a symphony of destruction, followed by the screeching of steel meeting steel.

The airbags deployed with a sudden, muffled pop, filling the interior with a cloud of white dust. The engine compartment, overwhelmed by the brutal force of the impact, shattered into pieces, and I noticed smoke rising from the crumpled engine block.

The collision violently pushed our vehicle off course, catapulting it a few meters to the left before finally coming to a stop in the middle of the highway we had just exited. Thankfully, no other cars were in sight at that moment, which averted a potentially catastrophic crash with another vehicle.

For a moment, I sat in shock, trying to comprehend what had just happened. Rita, who was unharmed like me, had exited the vehicle in a state of sheer panic. She began screaming at the top of her lungs, her hands trembling and her face twisted in fear. Despite the chaos around us, I managed to remain composed.

Stepping out of the vehicle, I was confronted with a scene of utter devastation. Fluids—oil, coolant, and transmission fluid—poured onto the road, creating a grim tableau of destruction. The once-proud vehicle, now a mangled wreck, sat immobile, with its engine block emitting a thin wisp of smoke.

As I cast my gaze towards the metal barrier, I was struck by the sight that underscored the sheer force of the impact. The barrier, previously a sturdy protector, now bore the scars of the collision, a testament to the power of the accident.

Shortly after the accident, a passing vehicle pulled over to help and called the police on our behalf. Moments later, an ambulance that was just driving by also stopped to check on us.

"We are passing by, but we decided to stop and see if everything is okay with the passengers!" one of the paramedics said.

"That's very kind of you! Thankfully, both of us are okay," I replied.

"Really?" they asked, surprised.

"Yes, indeed," I confirmed.

"Okay, just keep in mind that you may experience pain later. If that happens, please contact your doctor. For now, we will continue on our way."

"Thank you very much for your concern! It is greatly appreciated," I said.

The police acted swiftly and arrived shortly after the incident. Their efficiency was evident when they promptly called a nearby towing company on our behalf.

Fortunately, the towing company was located just a few kilometers away from the accident site. A short while after the police contacted them, they arrived to tow our vehicle to their yard.

We left the UK with our vehicle loaded with various items, including cartons of books that I was eager to keep in Germany. We needed a vehicle that was spacious enough to transport our belongings.

In the end, with the help of the towing company, we ordered a taxi that had sufficient space to accommodate a significant portion of our items. We collected the remaining belongings the next day.

The taxi ride home was uneventful. After a delay of about 90 minutes past our expected arrival time, we finally reached our destination, feeling a deep sense of relief.

Unfortunately, our beloved Renault Espace sustained extensive damage to the engine and other critical components in the front compartment, making it beyond economical repair. Our insurers reimbursed us for its assessed value at the time of the accident.

To facilitate our movements during our stay in Germany, we rented a vehicle to replace the one involved in the accident.

After almost two weeks in Germany, we returned to the UK by air.

***

Even as I write this testimony weeks after the accident, I find myself reflecting on the traumatic happening. I previously mentioned that I had a strange dream in which I was at the A&E, being prepared for what seemed to be an emergency surgery. While others may not share my perspective, the fact that the accident occurred shortly after the dream leads me to believe that the Evil One intended to harm me, but his plans were thwarted by the Lord, my Good Shepherd.

Naturally, one might wonder what caused the accident. While I am not an expert in motor accident research, I can confidently rule out mechanical failures from my perspective as a layperson.

In the UK, like in several other countries, vehicles are required to undergo regular inspections. The UK system, known as the MOT (Ministry of Transport test), is conducted annually and is quite thorough. Our vehicle had its last inspection just nine months before our unfortunate journey. Although I am not an expert in vehicle technology, I did not notice any mechanical issues as we set out on our trip—the tyres, brakes, and lights were all in good condition.

It is also worth mentioning that the accident was not caused by a third party. Although the road we traveled is typically quite busy, that stretch of highway seemed deserted at the time of the crash.

I can confidently rule out tiredness as a factor in the terrible crash. Driving long distances in a single day is not new to me; as an agency doctor, I am accustomed to traveling long distances to work at various locations. As I mentioned earlier, we made a rest stop about an hour before the accident, and at that time, I felt alert and vigilant.

I do not consume alcohol, and I had not taken any medications that could impair my alertness. Additionally, there were no disturbances from my fellow traveler.

The road I was driving on was also familiar to me, as we had traveled this stretch several times during our visits to Germany.

Ultimately, I attribute the crash to a combination of three factors: the darkness, the lack of highway lighting at the exit, and a miscalculation on my part that led me to continue driving straight instead of making a right turn.

When I take a moment to reflect on the various devastating outcomes that could have resulted from that horrific crash, I am truly in awe of the immense favor that God Almighty showed us on that occasion. To illustrate this clearly, I will present a few examples of the dire situations we narrowly escaped.

Death: The Lord saved us from the Angel of Death. One or both of us could have fallen victim to its sword. Without a doubt, it was the mighty hand of Almighty God that rescued us from the grasp of the Angel of Death. What power can the sword of the Grim Reaper hold in the presence of Almighty God?

Injury: Rita and I could have suffered various degrees and types of injuries. During my time as a hospital doctor, I encountered victims of road traffic accidents with injuries of differing severities. I recall one case of a young woman, around 19 years old, who sustained multiple injuries to her pelvis and both legs. She was in severe pain and was so incapacitated that it was heartbreaking to witness her suffering. Indeed, some victims were in such dire conditions that they fought for their lives over an extended period. Some injuries led to life-changing deformities, disabilities, and even paralysis.

Financial troubles: A lengthy hospital stay for both or either of us could have devastating financial implications, potentially resulting in bankruptcy and jeopardizing our ability to pay rent, which could lead to eviction from our home.

Imprisonment: As if the potential troubles I've just outlined weren't enough, I, as the driver of the crashed vehicle, could have faced imprisonment.

As a doctor in the UK, I have spent over 15 years serving as a prison doctor, working in various facilities across the country. During that period, I have encountered many inmates serving sentences for death by dangerous driving. One case that remains etched in my memory involved a lorry driver from Eastern Europe. He was delivering goods from mainland Europe to the UK and mistakenly forgot that, unlike in his native country where drivers drive on the right side of the road, in the UK, drivers drive on the left. This oversight led to an accident that resulted in a fatality.

Consequently, he was sentenced to several years in prison for death by dangerous driving.

I could indeed have faced the same fate if I had survived and Rita had not!

CHAPTER 17

For I am not ashamed of the Gospel of Christ

At the beginning of this book, I shared one of my favorite Bible verses: *"For we did not follow cunningly devised fables when we made known to you the power and coming of our Lord Jesus Christ, but were eyewitnesses of His majesty" (2 Peter 1:16).*

As I conclude my narrative, I would like to quote another Bible verse that I hold dear: *"For I am not ashamed of the gospel of Christ, for it is the power of God unto salvation to everyone who believes; to the Jew first, and also to the Greek" Romans 1:16.*

Romans 1:16 is attributed to Apostle Paul. The account of his conversion is well-known to many mainstream Christians. For those who may not be familiar with the circumstances of his conversion, here's a brief summary.

Initially known as Saul, Paul was a zealous follower of Jewish traditions. His strong beliefs led him to actively persecute Christians, whom he viewed as heretics. His dedication to this cause was so intense that he sought and obtained permission from the authorities in Jerusalem to travel to Damascus, where he intended to arrest anyone who called upon the name of the Lord.

Then, something truly extraordinary occurred: he had a life-altering encounter with the risen Lord. This experience was so profound that it completely transformed him. Instead of being a persecutor of the followers of the Cross, he became the most prominent advocate for the cause of the risen Lord, a transformation that starkly contrasts with his previous life.

In Romans 1:16, Paul, who once fiercely persecuted the Gospel, now boldly declares to the world that he is not ashamed of the Gospel of Christ.

I do not consider myself an authority in my mother tongue, Twi, which is spoken by the Akan people of Ghana. If I am not an expert in my own language, how can I claim to be proficient in English, a language I learned as a second language in school?

This brings me to the meaning of the word "ashamed," which is central to the verses I quoted earlier. While I am familiar with the term, I did some online research to confirm its meaning for the purpose of this discussion. This is the definition I found: feeling reluctant to do something due to fear of embarrassment or humiliation. To elaborate further , embarrassment involves feeling uneasy or uncomfortable, while humiliation refers to a loss of self-respect.

Thus, in Romans 1:16, Paul boldly asserts that he is neither embarrassed nor humiliated by his association with the gospel of Jesus Christ, and he does not feel a loss of self-respect.

Before I continue with my narration, I want to clarify one thing: I do not wish to compare myself to Paul, a giant of the Christian faith. While I refrain from equating my Christian experiences with his, I wholeheartedly adopt his words: "I am not ashamed of the Gospel of Christ."

How could I possibly feel embarrassment, humiliation, discomfort, or a loss of self-respect because of the Gospel of Jesus Christ? Yes indeed, how can I , in view of abundant goodness, kindness , mercies --- the list of the Lord's favours to me are endless--be ashamed of the Gospel of Christ?

While I don't claim to be perfect, I do not want to be categorized among ungrateful individuals, as referenced in a popular saying in my native language, Twi. I kindly ask the reader to bear with me for a moment as I reflect on this saying.

The Twi phrase "boni aye kae dabi" is challenging to translate directly into English. The first part, "boni aye," can be roughly understood as "ungrateful soul," while "kae dabi" means "don't forget the past." Together, the phrase can be translated to something like: "You ungrateful soul, remember the past."

Essentially, it expresses a sentiment similar to, "You ungrateful person, don't forget the kindness that was shown to you in the past." This phrase is typically uttered by those who feel aggrieved when someone seems to overlook the help they have received, which leaves the giver feeling unappreciated.

It's a situation many of us can relate to: you extend kindness only to find that it goes unacknowledged. Of course, some may exaggerate this feeling, using their past acts of kindness to make unreasonable demands on others. However, my focus is on genuine instances of ingratitude, where even a neutral observer would readily recognize the lack of appreciation being discussed.

I want to emphasize that, while I am far from perfect, I do not want to be considered among those who are ungrateful for the blessings we receive. I have already shared examples of the goodness and kindness of the Lord in my life in this book; the testimonies are just one part of a much larger narrative. I am truly grateful for the gift of life— the free air that fills my lungs, the water that quenches my thirst, the food that satisfies my hunger, and the beautiful creation I am privileged to admire. These are all gifts for which I feel immense gratitude.

In gratitude for the abundant goodness and kindness the Lord has bestowed upon me in the past, continues to bless me with in the present, and will undeniably provide in the future, I humbly make the following declaration:

I, Robert Kofi Peprah-Gyamfi, who was born in the humble surroundings of a little village called Mpintimpi, whose mother was not attended to by a professional mid-wife as she laboured under the scorching conditions of the African heat, whose hour, day, month and year of birth was not officially recorded; who grew up in the most impoverished of settings imaginable; whose impoverished parents could even not afford him a sandal until his teenage years—a situation which for a while led him to struggle to

differentiate between the left and right footwork; who at
the time of starting school adopted, in line with the trend
of time, the European first name Robert; whose education
was interrupted for two long years due to a mysterious
condition that afflicted his left ankle, during which he
was exposed to the most horrifying traditional treatment
regimes imaginable; who despite the humble settings of
his birth through the hand of Providence made it to medical school in Germany to train as a doctor; I am declaring
before the whole world that I am not ashamed of the Gospel
of Jesus Christ my Lord.

Yes, I declare to the whole world that I am not ashamed
to call myself the servant of Jesus Christ of Nazareth.
Please pardon me for being repetitive; this is intentional. It
is a way to drive home my point and underline the unwavering nature of my faith and commitment to Jesus Christ.

Yes, indeed, I want to reiterate: I am not ashamed to
call the Lord Jesus Christ of Nazareth, the King of Kings
and Lord of Lords—He who was, is, and evermore shall
be—my Master and the Lord of my life.

Yes, before I shut my big mouth for good, I want to take
this opportunity to declare loudly that I am not ashamed of
the Gospel of Christ! While others may find authority in
different sources, I know of no other power that brings such
freedom from the challenges of life than that of Almighty
God, Creator of Heaven and Earth, as revealed by my Lord
and Saviour Jesus Christ, the King of Kings and Lord of
Lords. Indeed, I am here to proclaim to the world that, in
my heart, the Lord Jesus Christ is the King of Kings and
Lord of Lords. He is the sinner's friend, the companion

of the friendless, the support for the poor, and a source of comfort for those who are depressed. He brings calm in the midst of turmoil and peace in times of conflict and trouble.

This statement is more than just a declaration; it reflects my deep conviction in the reality of the ever-present Savior, Jesus Christ, in my life. How could I claim otherwise when I have known Him as a personal friend—one who has protected me from countless dangers, intervened in my life on numerous occasions, guided me through seemingly insurmountable challenges, and provided a way for me when humanity had given up on me?

I foresee that my declaration of faith in the Risen Lord might prompt criticism from certain individuals. We live in a strange world where some who reject King Jesus not only leave the matter as it is but also ridicule and belittle anyone who dares to choose a different path.

By boldly proclaiming my allegiance to my Lord and King, I am likely to attract the ire of such individuals, who may label me in various negative ways.

Some may consider me delusional or suggest that I need psychiatric help for my belief in something they perceive as nonexistent. Others might dismiss me as unsophisticated, viewing me as someone with a childlike simplicity, eager to embrace any idea presented to him. Still, some may call me foolish, believing I am so naïve that I confuse fairy tales with reality.

To that, I declare:

Throughout my life, I have learned not to be swayed by what others say about me, whether in my presence or absence. People may mock me openly or speak behind my back, but their opinions do not affect me. They might call me various names, deride me, or scold me. Some may label me as stupid, silly, a lunatic, or an idiot. Ultimately, these views are their opinions, and they are their concerns, not mine.

Yes, indeed; no matter what others think of my open declaration of allegiance to my master, Jesus Christ, I will continue to confess Him openly as long as I have breath.

***

As I near the conclusion of this book, which captures the extraordinary Divine interventions I've experienced, I feel a strong urge to convey an important message, especially to those who are new in their faith journey.

While I am openly and enthusiastically testifying to the immeasurable grace and goodness of the Lord, my Master, I want to clarify that this does not mean I fully understand all of His ways and guidance in my life. I want to reiterate: just because I testify to the goodness of the Lord does not mean I comprehend every direction He takes in my life. In fact, there have been moments on my Christian journey when I have been puzzled by the paths He has led me down, leaving me wondering, "Good Lord, what is going on here?"

In those confusing and sometimes bizarre situations, I have drawn strength from the Bible passage : "For my thoughts are not your thoughts, neither are your ways my ways, saith the Lord. For as the heavens are higher than the earth, so are my ways higher than your ways, and my thoughts than your thoughts". Isaiah 55:8-9

"My ways are higher than your ways." Indeed, along my Christian walk, whenever I have struggled to understand the Lord's leading, I have found comfort in those words and have chosen to trust Him, assured that ultimately, everything will be well.

How can I, a mortal man who is here today and gone tomorrow, ever hope to fully comprehend the dealings of Almighty God with me specifically and with the world in general?

In His grace, the Lord has placed the soft matter we refer to as the brain within the protective cage of the skull to help us navigate our lives. Experts in brain research acknowledge that humanity has not been able to fully understand the workings of the brain. If our brains—a tool given to us by Almighty God for navigating life—cannot fully grasp their own functions, how can they dare to comprehend the workings of the Almighty and Everlasting God, the power behind the entire universe?

In light of this, I have learned to accept whatever comes my way without questioning. This acceptance has been especially important as I deal with the distressing medical condition of a close family member, which has presented us with a unique set of challenges. Out of respect for his medical confidentiality, I will not discuss the details further.

Over the years, we have earnestly sought the face of Almighty God, praying fervently for healing for him. Despite our unceasing prayers for his restoration, the condition has persisted. Does the apparent silence of the Almighty indicate His unconcern or indifference toward us?

Of course not!

Yes, I for sure I am not ashamed of Christ Jesus, my Lord and wholeheartedly recommend Him to the world. So dear Reader, if you haven't already, I encourage you to invite the Lord into your life.

"Here I am! I stand at the door and knock. If anyone hears my voice and opens the door, I will come in and eat with that person, and they with me." Revelation 3:20

This is, of course, a voluntary act. Jesus, our Lord, respects your freedom of choice and does not impose Himself on anyone. Your decision is yours to make. Please remember, today is your opportunity for salvation; tomorrow could be too late.

If you have any questions or need support, don't hesitate to reach out to me through the email on the copyright page. I'm here to assist you. Additionally, I encourage you to find a Bible-believing church in your area for fellowship. You are not alone on this incredible journey!

PHOTO REPORT

I am sharing photos that illustrate the extent of the damage to our vehicle from the terrible crash.

Our badly damaged Renault Espace on a tow truck.

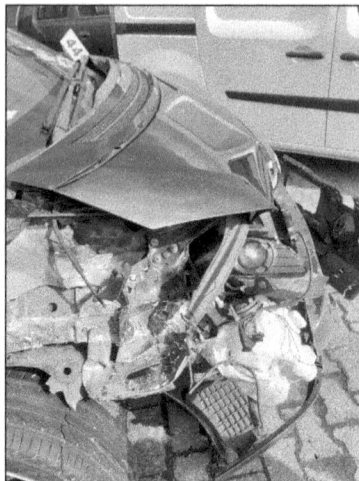

The front of the vehicle suffered major damage.

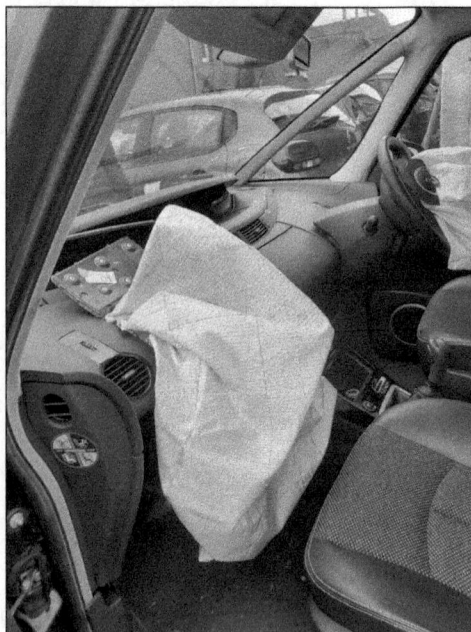

The impact of the collision triggered the deployment of both airbags.

www.ingramcontent.com/pod-product-compliance
Lightning Source LLC
Chambersburg PA
CBHW071134090426
42736CB00012B/2117